The 20% Rule®

How to ensure your small business is safe,
sustainable and profitable

The 20% Rule®

Copyright © Catherine Gladwyn 2021

ISBN 978-1-912009-45-9

First published by Compass-Publishing in 2020

Set and designed by The Book Refinery Ltd
www.thebookrefinery.com

Edited by Jo Watson
www.agoodwriteup.com

A catalogue copy of this book is available from the British Library.

What People are Saying about The 20% Rule®

"If a book could speak, this one would say "Oi! I'm talking to you"..

Because it really was. And not just me personally, but every single service based business owner.

I love Catherine's tone. She's lighthearted but you KNOW she's serious. She's not messing about – you need to heed her advice and make changes in your business to ensure it's safe, sustainable and profitable.

This is the book I wish I'd read at the start of my business journey. And yet it still makes so much sense to me, almost 9 years into being a business owner.

Sit up, get it read and take note... You won't be sorry if you do, but I can promise you, you'll be missing out if you don't."

– Jo Francis – Facebook Ads Specialist

"I really didn't want to use the words 'no-nonsense' in this review of Catherine Gladwyn's second book, the follow-up to her hugely successful and award-winning 'How to be a VA'. However, there really is no other way to describe the advice she imparts in this fantastic business book. Catherine's no-nonsense attitude towards running a business is so refreshing in the somewhat over-populated world of small business reading.

I have read a LOT of business books since looking to start my own business almost three years ago. Many have contained useful advice, interesting points of view and thought-provoking commentary that has made me question and evaluate my own business practice. Many have not. The 20% Rule® is, I think, the first book of this kind that I KNOW I will use as a bible for my business, despite it being fairly established and successful already. It's all well and good having miraculous mornings, but you won't reach your full potential without the actionable, no-nonsense (there, I've said it again) advice that Catherine gives here.

If you're new in business, or are looking to start up, this book is an absolute must to add to your collection. In fact, don't bother with a collection; you won't need anything else once you've read this and actioned Catherine's advice. As well as explaining The 20% Rule® and how it will preserve your business, she goes into great detail about many other aspects of starting and running a sustainable business, including the foundations you need to put in place, pricing, marketing and many of the myths that she believes hinder business owners from becoming truly successful.

Full of practical advice and anecdotal evidence, Catherine's book is so far from the dry 'how to....' business books that end up half-read and gathering dust on the shelf. Reading it feels like having a chat with a mate who really knows her shizzle when it comes to running a business and you just know that if you follow the well thought-out action points throughout the book, you'll make her proud and she'll always be there cheering you on.

Whether you're thinking of starting a business, already up and running, or well into your self-employed journey, you need this book. The 20% Rule® makes so much sense and I'd call Catherine Gladwyn a genius, but we don't want her head to explode (read the book to find out why!)."

– Kelly Kemp – Creative Tech

"I am now two years into my business and although it is doing well, there are areas we can always improve on. This book didn't fail to deliver. It's like a mini-business course all in one book. I had a notebook beside me and was frantically taking notes on tips I know will help massively in my business to take it to the next level. I have always been aware that it is so important to have solid foundations in place in a business and Catherine provides all the steps required in order to ensure these are implemented. The 20% Rule® was also something I had heard Catherine mention in her membership group for many months and it is always at the back of my mind when taking on new clients. It is so important for sustainability.

I highly recommend this book to any service-based business owners. It has all the information you need, written in an easy to read style (and with Catherine's sense of humour) with nuggets of valuable information.

It's like having her on my shoulder while reading it!

It is definitely a business book must-have."

– Emma Rowley – Virtual Assistant

Catherine is the multi-award winning bestselling author of How to be a Virtual Assistant.

2019 and 2020 Winner of VAVA Awards ~ 'Best Book for Virtual Assistants'

2019 and 2020 Amazon Bestseller ~ Category: Small Business and Entrepreneurship

2018, 2019 and 2020 Amazon Bestseller ~ Category: Home-Based Business Book

2019 Mentioned in The Guardian ~ 'How I Spend It'

2018 The Independent Newspaper, listed as ~ One of Ten Best Business Books Written by Women

Featured In:

The Guardian, Cosmopolitan, Forbes, The Independent, Metro, Mail Online

Dedicated to

Chloe and Antony

Contents

About

~

Back in 2010, I was managing a team of eleven administrators and working as a PA to a director for a national charity. It was great. I had loads to do and could do it all incredibly well, but then things suddenly started to get really difficult. Tasks I'd previously done every day I could no longer remember how to do. I'd have a meeting with someone in the morning, then an hour later, I'd forget everything that had been said. Sometimes, I'd even forget that I'd had a meeting in the first place.

By 2011, I was growing increasingly convinced that something wasn't quite right. Hell, I'd lived with myself for 34 years, so I knew that things were a bit weird. My memory was going, my eyesight was poor, I was exhausted all the time, and my periods had stopped. I was sweating like mad at night and there were other symptoms, too, but like I say, my memory was fading fast, and I kept forgetting what they were.

In 2012, after a year of trying to convince my GP that I wasn't bloody stressed and wasn't going through early menopause, I knew that a diagnosis of something more sinister was on the way. Sure enough, I was diagnosed with a tumour in my pituitary gland. As you'll know, the pituitary gland sits at the base of your brain and basically controls almost every facet of your body and your everyday life. It's the size of a pea but by god that bugger is not to be messed with. It's where our hormones sit and play all day, but my tumour was having its own fun; stopping lots of different hormones from doing their thing in trying to keep me healthy and alive.

In November 2012, I had neurosurgery. The surgeon's plan was to remove the tumour. It suddenly dawned on me how real all of this was.

The surgery was successful, and I spent the next year or two being incredibly grateful for life, laughter and everything I had, which included spending every day with my partner and my beautiful daughter.

Fast-track to 2014, and I could feel that something wasn't quite right again. I felt off-balance – in all senses. It was like when you step out of a lift and it takes a while to find your centre, or when you're a little hungry and feel a bit faint. Then, the night sweats started, and my speech became affected as I couldn't remember or articulate words easily at all. I remember having an interview for a promotion with my then employers. I was earmarked for the job as the interviewers knew me and loved my work, but I didn't get the job as I couldn't recall anything at all in the interview. The panel all sat there, open mouthed, wondering what the hell was wrong with me.

You guessed it; the bugger was back! Tumour: Take Two.

In June 2014, I had Gamma Knife Radiotherapy in London. Sounds lovely, doesn't it? It's just one targeted and intense 'zap' to the tumour, as opposed to five zap-filled days a week for five weeks. I was lucky to have the opportunity to undertake this procedure, and I feel for anyone who has to do the five-week treatment.

Following my procedure, life was a little different. I'd gone on to misplace or completely lose a few hormones, and parts of my brain didn't work as well as they probably should have done, but in a way, I was kind of glad it all happened, as I don't think I'd be where I am today without that experience.

In 2016, I took the 'life's too short' approach and changed my life to accommodate my rare disease by becoming a business owner, making myself happier and healthier than I ever had been as an employee. Four years on, in a very successful business, I continue to lose a few hormones from time to time and have also kept things exciting by developing a potentially fatal condition called Addison's Disease! But I'm here. And I'm writing this book. If you haven't figured out 'why' just yet, you will.

To sum up my condition, my pituitary gland no longer talks to my adrenal glands – which is a bit awkward – and so my body doesn't produce any Cortisol. I have to take fake Cortisol three times a day just to keep me alive. Stress can kill me, because my body can't and/or won't release Cortisol to cope with it. Sadly, this even includes 'good' stress – so no sending me massive gifts or surprising me with balloons (just in case you were thinking about it)! With Addison's Disease comes severe fatigue and other stuff not even worth mentioning, but being my own boss enables me to manage all of that in a way that would be impossible if I was an employee. I told you this was going somewhere.

I had all the fear you'd expect from making that leap from employee to business owner.

What if I don't make any money?

What about a pension? (This was a ridiculous question as I didn't have one anyway, but your brain doesn't often care about being rational, does it?)

What if I'm not successful?

How will this affect my daughter?

What if I get ill again?

I had so many questions – and I could probably fill a book with them alone – but ultimately, I only had one thought to answer them all…

If I stay in my job, one day it will literally kill me.

Feeling motivated, yet???

I made my journey as a business owner work because not only was it what I wanted, but it was what I needed. I was also continuously worried that the tumour would come back for a third time. Things happen in threes, as they say.

In September 2019, the NHS agreed for me to have an MRI scan. To their surprise, but not to mine, my tumour was indeed back for a third time. It was growing, and fast. In the words of the consultant, there was an *imminent* need to get me into surgery. I had less than four weeks to get things ready.

I had no life insurance or critical illness cover, as it was too expensive because of my already recurring tumour and because of my Addison's Disease, too.

There was no way I was losing my business, but there was also no way I could not have the surgery. A four-month recovery period, though…

But, I was prepared, because I knew this day would come.

And now? I want to share with you how you too can prepare to ensure that your business is safe, sustainable and profitable – even when life gets in the way.

Ready? Let's do this...

Introduction

~

Thank you for buying my book. I hope it wasn't lent to you by someone else who bought it, because now I'm down a tenner, if that's the case!

Anyway, if you want to build a safe, sustainable and profitable business, I believe you're in the right place.

People come to me at various stages of their business development and I have seen enormous change in people's profits and longevity when they follow The 20% Rule®.

All too often, business owners are trying to run before they can walk. They want the freedom that being a business owner can bring (having a spontaneous day out with the kids, for example), but often don't realise the sacrifice that's needed.

What follows in this book are things I do in my own business and / or things I have advised others to do through my mentoring. All of those things have seen real results. Everything has been tested.

You can implement just some of the advice, if you wish, but for full rewards, I'd suggest full commitment.

You're going to need tenacity and must never let fear dictate your feast.

Safe: Your business is ready for when life gets in the way.

Sustainable: Your business has longevity and you've proved you're no 'one hit wonder'. People need what you do – and you're seen as the go-to expert.

Profitable: You're making and saving money consistently every month and investing in your business as you do it.

Becoming the Expert

Be known for what you do

~

Throughout this book, I'll encourage you to become known as the expert in your field, so that when someone needs your specific services, the first person they'll think of is you.

I dismiss the need for an 'ideal client avatar'. Controversial, right? It'll all make sense, I promise.

When I started limiting my offering in my Virtual Assistant business to just two main services, marketing became so easy and I became known for what I did, rather than for being 'just another' Virtual Assistant.

Of course, there were other elements to getting to this stage. It wasn't just a case of changing my bio and suddenly being an expert just because I'd used that word.

You need to become *known* for what you do. That's the goal.

But how?

As with anything, it takes time to get to that stage of people automatically thinking of you when the topic of your services comes up. The good news is that it doesn't involve you having to give things away for free for you to get there.

Becoming the expert is actually easier when you are known for *what* you do and not *who* you serve. If you're only known for who you work with, how are you going to get strong leads, strong referrals and strong recommendations? It's great being liked by people, but 'Ohhhh Catherine's lovely' doesn't get me any work. 'Catherine's lovely, and she knows all about XY and Z' *does.*

Let's get you to that point. Even if your name's not Catherine.

The Foundations

The perks of being your own boss only come into play if you have a business that's giving you an income

~

From my experience of running my own business – and tripping up along the way more than a handful of times in the early days – I have found that there are a few fundamental things you need in place *before* you can really move forward to create a safe, sustainable and profitable business that you're proud of. You may already be doing some of them. If that's the case, feel like a hero at this point and dust off that cape.

I urge you not to overlook any of what follows, though, because as a client once said to me…

> *'I often wonder where I'd be now if I'd stayed with my coach four years ago and followed on with her advice. I've made lots of costly mistakes and now find myself doing everything she was trying to get me to do in the first place.'*

Productivity

You are every department for your business, so you need to be productive and set boundaries for yourself. Some people find getting dressed for the day works well (I'm not one of those people, by the way). Some people find things like time-blocking works for them. I work well with a daily to-do list. Not only does it feel great as you mark things off, but you also get to see what you've achieved in that day. "Have a productive day" – tick!

I've also found little things like not putting the washing on during the day, not cleaning the sink in the kitchen, or not agreeing to meet up with people more than once in a week all help to keep me focused, but the biggest thing for me was seeing every hour of my life as my hourly rate.

It may take time to find what works for you but consider every hour as money. So, that two-hour lunch with your best mate who's on annual leave from their employed job (and is therefore getting paid to drink wine with you right now) is seen as two hours of your time where you've lost money, or two hours you'll have to work extra that evening outside of your usual working day to make up the loss. Watch it start to add up and start spending your time wisely.

Start now with your planning…

Before you throw that laptop into a drawer or power-down your PC, write tomorrow's to-do list. That way, you know what's expected of you as soon as you get into the 'office' the next day. You can start the day focused, but you can also finish your day today knowing that tomorrow is planned out and so you don't need to keep anything in your head tonight.

It also stops that 'Oh, I must remember to do that' feeling when you wake at 4am for that trip to the bathroom! If you're still young, I appreciate you probably won't understand that concept, just yet. Sleep well.

Stay focused

A common question from business owners old and new is, *'How do you stay focused when you're a business owner?'*

Well, for starters, don't post that question on Facebook and wait for the replies!

Sometimes we can be our own worst enemies. Even without realising, we can put barriers in our own way. It's habitual.

Did you know that we probably only earn money for around 3 or 4 hours a day, even if we're sitting in the office for 8 hours? There are so many distractions. I use a piece of software to track the time it takes to do everything that I actually need to do, and I recommend you use such tech, too. I think you'll be really surprised that your numb bum is only bringing in four hours' worth of paid work most days. It's not a good surprise, I'll give you that, but it'll get you focused!

But what's distracting us?

- Getting stuck in an argument online – or is that just me?

- You started scrolling through Facebook and saw that Jennie has updated her profile picture of herself with a new bloke, but you didn't even know the old bloke had gone, so now you're in a stalking frenzy to find out what happened with Jennie and the first bloke she was living with. Who got the house? He was nice, wasn't he... Oh, look at his Mum, she looks lovely... Honestly, Jennie, why did you leave him?

- You saw a shiny new offer for a 5 day challenge that you can do right now to instantaneously boost your business, so you signed up and then completely forgot about the challenges you have that are relevant in the here and now.

Sound a little bit familiar?

I get distracted too from time to time. We all do.

Here are some things I do to help me be more productive during my working day. Some of them may really help you.

Start the day

Don't worry, I'm not going to suggest you start your day with a 15-mile run, an hour of yoga, or a turmeric broccoli squash smoothie. My suggestion is much easier to digest than that.

Often having too much on your to-do list can create a sense of panic. Panic can then make you feel overwhelmed, and then overwhelm makes us panic even more, and... (I could add so many more words to my book by repeating myself here, but you get the idea). Panic wastes time and distracts your full attention from the task in hand, so if we can find a way to remove the panic, we can become more productive and focused.

Try starting every day with a small daily to-do list. Not an open-ended one or a weekly one – a daily list. Perhaps four or five things on there per day, maximum. That way, you can focus on just a few tasks that need doing before the day is out. It removes overwhelm and gets rid of the need to prioritise. Plus, the shorter the list, the more likely it'll be you can get away earlier from your productive day and find out why Jennie left that first bloke after all! Tick!

Focus on bringing the money in

Make your initial tasks of the day those that will bring the money in. This way, it's impossible to end your day feeling like you've been 'unproductive'.

For example:

- Respond to potential new client enquiries

- Provide quotes or proposals for work

- Throw some social media posts out for the day, so that they can work for you whilst you're working

- Make contact with past or existing clients (good customer service leads to long-term relationships)
- Complete outstanding work so that you can send final invoices

Have a notepad

Do you ever start a task and think, *'Ooh, I must remember to do this'* or *'Aah, I better just quickly do this other thing before I forget'...?*

I've lost days ooh-ing and aah-ing, and not always in a good way!

But did you know, when you stop a task to do something else, it takes an average of 23 minutes to refocus and get on with the original task? Not great for time management and productivity, is it? Since finding out that little stat I've told my other half to get his endless deliveries from Amazon sent to his work address, so I'm not constantly up and down the damn stairs all day, literally signing my life away.

To avoid me going off track and trying to multitask too much, I have a notebook next to me all day. I jot down those little things and 'other' tasks that come into my head, so I don't have to try and remember them later on. If I have time after the day is done, I can get on with those tasks, or I can add them to tomorrow's to-do list instead.

Social media distractions

Is there a way to avoid the distractions of social media without locking yourself in a cellar with a packet of biscuits?

Yes, there is! And, even better, you can still have the biscuits!

It's all simply about limiting your time, but I know that's easier said than done, so here are a few things you can do to stop Facebook (other platforms are available) from taking over your life:

1. Log out of the platform on your laptop / PC and remove the automatic password fill. This creates an extra barrier to you getting onto the platform in a mindless click.

2. Remove the app from your phone, thus making your only way of getting social online via the laptop / PC – and that isn't so easy now you've done number 1!

3. If you can't remove the app from your phone, get an app blocker. I have mine set to come on from 12:00 until 14:00 so I can break properly for lunch, and from 20:00 until 07:00 so I can sleep well. Sleep is vital.

4. Set a timer. Before you go online, set a timer and, as I said initially, limit your time on there/out there. Perhaps 10-minute bursts of scrolling/supposing/snooping?

Networking (face to face)

Possibly a controversial topic, but are those networking events really benefiting you and your business, or are they like a cup of tea? Warm and comforting at first, but goes cold quickly and leaves a bitter aftertaste?

Keep reading on and weigh up the pros and cons.

Consider how much it's costing you in all senses by travelling to the venue, spending time there, purchasing refreshments, paying for entry (whether it's a one-off or an annual cost), travelling back home, then trying to 'get back into' work (as referred to earlier)!

An example:

Let's say your hourly rate is £50. It takes 30 minutes to travel to the event, then you're there for two hours, and then it's 30 minutes to travel back home – that's cost you £150. You've then got to factor in the cost of the event and any add-ons, so we're easily heading into £200 territory now, aren't we?

Will you recoup that cost somewhere down the line as a result of attending?

Go for a second time and we're looking at a £400 expense. Yes, you may not be paying that money out, but you're not bringing it in either, are you?

So, even if you do get business from it eventually, is all that expense in the past ever going to be fully recouped through networking? It's worth pondering.

I compare it (a little) to gambling. Yes, you've just won £80 on a horse, but you spent £360 on bets. You therefore didn't win £80 – you lost £280.

The world is your oyster, so spend a little time looking at online networking instead. The world is now fully set up for this, so no excuses.

There's no science to it. Simply connect, engage, show interest, join debates and enjoy it. You have to enjoy it if you're committing to this stuff. Six months of heavy, focused, consistent online networking – that doesn't cost you any additional extras in time or money – will really start working for you (if networking is your thing, of course).

Know how much you need to earn

I am really surprised when I ask business owners under my mentorship, *'How much do you need to earn to make your business work for you?'* and the reply is, *'I don't know'*.

Wait!

If you don't know how much you need to earn, how do you know how much to charge? How do you know you're not facing famine every month? How do you know your bills can be paid? How do you know if the business is even viable?

It's imperative that you know what your outgoings are every month and how much you need to earn to cover them and to make a nice healthy profit that gives you the life you want.

When it comes to outgoings, you might want to consider letting some things go, early doors. The luxuries can come later. Little cuts make a big difference. For example, that four-weekly haircut… can it be done every six weeks instead?

Are you using the cheapest energy supplier? Is anyone actually watching those extra channels you're paying for? Do you need all those added extras on your mobile phone contract? Check them all out.

Once you know how much you need to bring in each month, add a couple of hundred to that figure to cover you for a savings account. You'll need a holiday, and I know all too well how important it is to have funds ready to cover any periods when you're unwell! I cover more on this in the Emergency Planning chapter.

Messaging

Ensure your messaging is clear and consistent across all social media channels, your website and anywhere else you display a logo, bio and/or a summary of your business and its services. If people find you in one place and the services you offer differ elsewhere in your online presence, they're not going to know what's most current, or indeed where your expertise really does lie. It doesn't look great and, at best, you'll come across as a Jack of all Trades. If so, potential clients will find it easier to go off and find someone who's definitely focused on what they're looking for.

Set a reminder in your calendar now to check your messaging every six months.

Go on, I'll wait.

Prices

People should not have to get in touch with you to find out what their investment might be should they want to work with you.

Ensure your rates are clear and unambiguous. Don't invite people to get in touch for a price. This is imperative so don't skip this step.

Some businesses will give a 'price from' and that's great if there's no exact figure, but you should also consider displaying a top-end price so that people know their maximum investment if/when they choose you.

Ensure your services are clear and easy to understand. Ask a business owner from a different field to take a look to ensure you're not using any jargon or confusing people with offers. Please avoid asking a friend or family member who doesn't run their own business because – as you know – they'll mean well but likely have no experience how business works!

Still think your services are too broad to advertise set prices? Perhaps it's time to consider offering fixed price packages. This is much more appealing to people and stops them looking around elsewhere!

Boundaries

Define your boundaries from the start and consider adding them to your terms and conditions / client contracts. For example, I state my working hours and make it clear that outside of this is family time. In other words, you can call me, but don't expect me to answer!

I also only communicate with my clients via email or via pre-arranged calls – which are charged. If a client messages me on a social messenger app at any time of the day, even if it falls within my working hours, I ask them to email me. I can't receive work via a messenger system, because I forget to action it or add it to my lists… it's not how I want to work.

Another controversial point, but I do not find meeting face-to-face to be an efficient way to run my business, and I find that phonecalls take longer than communicating by email, so I sway people away from those things by letting them know that all calls and face to face meetings are charged at my hourly rate. People soon lose that 'need' to talk to you on the phone or in person – thus freeing up much more of your time.

Consider what you do *and do not* want to do in your role, and remember that the first time you let those boundaries be pushed, you're essentially telling that person it's ok to do it all the time.

People will treat you how you allow them to treat you. Say nothing, though, and they don't know. People can't read your thoughts. You cannot complain that a client is doing x, y and z unless you've told that client you do not accept it. This is your responsibility, and will save you and your clients a lot of hassle.

Website

I've seen 'advice' online where people say things like, *"Don't worry about having a website, you can just use social media to promote your business."*

That would mean all of your marketing is free! Result.

If only it was that easy...

Whilst social media platforms might be free, they're not *yours* – and that's the crucial thing here. You're just a guest, and you may be classed as unwelcome at any time. Social media is better used as a way to direct people to your website.

You've heard people say how impossible it is to contact Facebook, Instagram, LinkedIn etc., when something goes wrong, haven't you? I've heard that too, but I have also witnessed fellow online business owners lose their business accounts through hacking attacks or by accidentally flouting the endless list of terms and conditions. They never get their profiles back! You can threaten to boycott Mark Zuckerberg all you like – but you're not going to put him out of business, and even if you tried… he doesn't care!

With that loss of your social media presence comes the loss of the audience you've built up and the relationships you've developed. You'll never find them all again, and so you'll effectively have to start your marketing from scratch. Get a website!

When was the last time you spent money with someone/on something that only had a social media profile? Unless we know them personally, we seek out a website. Without one, we feel like our transaction may not even be safe. Don't make people doubt you.

A website is yours for keeps. It's somewhere people in this busy world can go to find out all about you and what it is you can do for them. A website answers their FAQs and gives them a place to find out how much it's going to cost them to invest in you. Potential clients will be looking at your website from mobiles, laptops and computers at all times throughout the day and night. It's your 24/7 shop front. It's a great place to store testimonials, too.

As a service-based business owner, your target audience are likely to be people who are busy in their business, and therefore too busy to be doing or learning the things you can do for them instead. They don't have time to scroll through endless posts on social media trying to find out how to get in touch with you, how much you charge, and what it is you actually do.

People don't want an awkward conversation on the phone with you only to find out you're out of their price range, or you're not a good fit, or the services they assumed you provide… you actually don't. Potential clients want to find out all of that information quickly and have ease of access to get in touch with you to say *let's work together*. They can only do that if you have it all in one safe place – your website.

Don't make it difficult for people to spend money with you. Make it easy.

Excuses

Now, let's quit with the excuses, shall we? If you can't do something, your competitors will.

How much is this costing me?

I couldn't spend any time today on my marketing as my niece is over from Australia and lunch just got out of hand…

If that scenario sounds familiar, please make sure that if you're enjoying the perks of being a business owner, your business gives you the income you need to be able to take the time off in the first place.

Could you have gone on an all-day lunch if you were employed? The perks of being your own boss only come into play if you have a profitable business. Until then, your spare time isn't spare – it's business.

Work-life balance is fine, of course, but not if it sacrifices your business as a result. Put the work in now, and you won't have to, later. Take shorter lunches until then.

I can't speak for your niece, but if she can take the time off for a long lunch – or to come over from an entirely different country – then either she's worked hard to build a profitable business, or she's employed. You're not. You don't get paid for your time off. Remember that.

If you want this business malarkey to work out for you, you need to concentrate on your goal and manage your time so that you can build a business that's safe, sustainable and profitable.

Always ask yourself, *how much is this costing me?*

How to say 'No'

Learning how to say no in business is probably one of the hardest things you'll have to do. Saying no when someone wants a discount, saying no when someone wants to meet in person and you don't feel it's necessary, and saying no when you don't want/can't work with that potential new client (for whatever reason).

It's scary, especially because you don't want to be without money and you don't want to go back to being employed now you've had the taste of being your own boss, do you?

However, there are always times when you're going to have to say No. They could be because

- You're at capacity

- You can't do the task being asked of you

- It's not something you enjoy

- You know the person asking is a bloody nightmare

My secret tip? Say 'no' and then pause. You'll naturally try to fill the silence – but fight it.

One thing a friend said to me once was, *'You don't have to explain yourself to anyone. If it's no, it's no'*. I remember this constantly.

You just need to say 'No'. Nothing else.

Email checking

Seriously, this bit had to be added to the book quite late on as I couldn't believe people don't do this anyway! Get into the habit of checking your emails at least twice a day – including your spam or junk folders. This is how most of the world communicates now – online. If you're not checking your emails, then you can guarantee your competitors are – and they'll also be replying in a timely manner, too. I was gobsmacked to find that some business owners, whose contact pages actively ask people to email them, aren't checking their inbox every day! This needs to be a regular thing you do. Just not every five minutes.

Madness.

The 20% Rule®

No one client should take up more than 20% of your time – or your income

~

Why? Well what if you lost them? What if they no longer needed you? What if their own business collapsed?

What if there's been a clash of personalities? What if somebody else has come along offering everything you do plus another wonderful thing that they need? What if they receive an unexpectedly high tax bill and can't afford you?

I start most of those sentences with 'what if', but all of them are real examples from real people I have mentored. I've even experienced some of them myself.

When you run your own business, things could all change overnight for you – quite easily.

If it's hard to imagine, how about a learning from a newsworthy example – one you can Google and find the case studies about in seconds. Here we go:

Not too long ago, Honda announced it was going to close its UK manufacturing plant in Swindon, Wiltshire (my hometown). In the run up to that closure, many small businesses who had supplied services to Honda over the years went out of business; caterers, cleaners, small parts suppliers, delivery companies etc., because they relied only – or too heavily – on Honda for their income. And it stopped coming in.

It was the same when Carillion closed down in the UK. Many small businesses folded because they relied on Carillion for all – or too much – of their income.

Sometimes, those big contracts seem irresistible, don't they? The big-name branding, the large and regular payments… If you have one client responsible for all or most of your income, though, your business is not safe, is not sustainable, and could very quickly prove not very profitable.

It's not just about if they go bust, either. You know what it's like when you're working closely with somebody; personalities clash and you rub each other up the wrong way. Quite quickly, a relationship can go sour – even if they're currently a 'mate' who would 'never leave' you.

That time-zapping singular client can also forget that you're their equal, and start seeing you as an employee – as somebody at their beck and call to support them. Whilst you might enjoy that initially because the money is nice, I can almost guarantee that it will grate on you eventually and you'll be trying all you can to 'manage them out' of your life.

But how can you achieve that? You've let your marketing go, you've got very little time free, and you really don't know how to find those clients anymore because you've been so busy absorbing yourself in someone else's business. Honestly, this is more like being employed again, isn't it?

Can you turn it around, though?

Absolutely.

I'm here to share my experiences of being in business and to help you achieve and sustain my 20% Rule® with all the things I do to keep my business safe, sustainable and profitable – no matter what life throws your way.

In March 2020, I applied for the trademark for the phrase, The 20% Rule®, in readiness for this book. I'd already been working to the rule myself for a few years, though. Here's why:

When I started my business a few years ago, I got clients relatively quickly. One was a friend and one was somebody who I worked with indirectly via my previous employers. It wasn't long before I was almost replacing my full-time income with her freelance work and, so, fed up to the back teeth of being stressed, ill and constantly frustrated as an employee, I left work on my quest to become a full-time work from home Virtual Assistant.

I had all the fears people openly talk about; what if I fail/ if people laugh at me/ if I go broke, etc.

I continued building my business, though, and I soon took on another local client alongside the initial two. *'Great! This is going fab, I'm now almost earning what I did when I was employed – but I'm actually enjoying it'*, I thought to myself.

However, one of those clients was contributing over 50% of my income, and she also took up a bulk of my time, primarily because I needed to travel to her offices and I wasn't (at the time) charging for that. I used to do bookkeeping and general office management for her on a 'safe' retained basis. This client had a turnover of half a million pounds a year, so there would be no problems with her paying me. I'd struck gold, in my opinion; profitable client, retainer contract, majority of employed income covered – tick, tick, tick.

However, that one client also relied heavily on one client herself! I'd say about 85% of her income and enviable turnover (which, by the way, shouldn't ever be confused with profit) was coming from one organisation.

Despite appearing Instagram perfect in her business, this six-figure business owner fell out with her largest client and, whilst she was still invited to tender for jobs every so often, she stopped winning them. With that came a huge decrease to her income. Her employed staff were laid off, but I was kept on for a little while because she desperately needed to get payments in from endless outstanding invoices.

I think part of me knew that either *I* needed a miracle or *she* did. She had two mortgages up to her ears, she had a long lease on her offices, she drove the best cars and she wore the best clothes. I was sure she'd get another client or two soon, but all I could see was panic.

It suddenly dawned on me how quickly things can change and that you're never EVER safe in someone else's hands.

I started backing off a little bit and stopped travelling to her offices – using the time instead to work on my own business and get my name out there more to promote myself to others. I ramped up my social media marketing, found some face to face networking events to go to on my days off (they were pointless), I made my website clearer, I utilised all the free advertising space I could find, and I got in touch with everyone who had ever expressed an interest in my services and anyone who had used my services ad hoc previously. I also reminded friends and family what I did and thanked them for their ongoing support. I kept contacting new people and showing up online every day.

Then, the call from my client came. My hours would need to be drastically reduced. There went my income.

My hard work was starting to pay off a little, but I still had to go back to employment.

I got myself a temporary job as a PA and I hated every long, mundane and unfulfilling second of it; not just returning to an office with restrictions on my time, but being told how to speak, behave, dress…

As I walked out of that building every day, I swore I would never go back to being permanently employed and that I would do everything I could to build a safe, sustainable and profitable business for myself.

You may have heard self-employed people talk about 'feast or famine' as if it's a natural thing for us to go through and as if there's nothing we can do about it.

*'The **feast** or **famine cycle** is what happens when a business owner lacks control of their turnover / profits, because of ineffective or non-existent marketing. It's impossible to build a successful business – until you break that cycle.'*

– Jim Connolly

I was NOT going to go back to employment every few months / years because of the famine that had happened previously. I needed to break the cycle. There are many business owners who consistently go through feast, so why should anyone ever have to constantly worry about going through the uncertainty of famine; being uncomfortable or financially stressed?

I hadn't been marketing my business as much as I could have done because I was a new business owner and there wasn't really any adequate guidance out there at the time. I couldn't find anyone who was doing what I was doing (and doing it really well) so I had nobody to learn from.

I attempted to work on my business whilst in temporary employment, but I couldn't access Gmail on their server, so my plans there were scuppered. I had to work in the evenings, at weekends and during my lunch break, but, if something is worth having, then the hard work and long hours need to be put in. This is where I see people fall down, regularly.

On my first day 'back at work', I'd stood outside the building and phoned my other half, saying quite simply, *"I don't want to do this"*. But I had to. I'm quite glad I did, actually, because it made me determined to never put myself through this again.

Within a few weeks of being in that job, I got a call from somebody I had never even spoken to before, saying they'd seen me online. They liked my presence and felt I stood out in my field. They'd already done a bit of stalking and mentioned that everything I'd listed as services I provide on my website were things they'd need help with. After a couple more calls we started working together and, because I'd been constantly honing my marketing and online presence (having by then ditched face to face networking completely), I was able to leave the employed job within another 8 weeks.

I had literally been spending every spare moment I had finding extra clients, by telling everybody and anybody what it was I could do, how I could help them, and how much it would cost them. I wasn't afraid to show people how I could make their life easier with what is a relatively small investment.

Even though my main goal was to create the working life I wanted, I learned to always let clients know that I enjoy working with them. I love what I do and tell them that their reputation is always as important to me as my own. I think, certainly in those early days, that emanated from me – and drew people to me.

It was from this point that I decided that I would not allow any one client to take up more than 20% of my time. Some clients today take up 10%, some take up 5%, but nobody takes up more than 20% – ever. Some days a client needs more than others and that's absolutely fine, but generally speaking, nothing over 20% of my time – and no one client being responsible for more than 20% of my income, either.

I mentor a lot of people who aren't exactly 'there' yet. Some have one or two clients taking up far too much of their time, and this means that their business isn't safe, isn't sustainable, and could very quickly become less than profitable. Through my mentoring, we work on this.

Through this book, we'll work on it, too, but what I can't do is implement anything for you. I can show you how and tell you why, but then you've got to do the hard work yourself.

Know Your Hourly Rate

What is your time worth?

~

Many business owners work on an hourly rate, but some offer prices as packages or subscriptions. It's going to be really useful for various parts of this book if you work out what your hourly rate is.

Or, to put it another way, what is your time worth?

Here are some questions and tips for determining your hourly rate:

- What do you need to earn?

- What are your expenses?

- What additional expenses might there be?

- Add 30% for taxes and to cover holidays, sickness and emergencies

- Consider what your billable hours will likely be per week

- Do some market research on people within your sector

- Don't sell yourself short

Remember, if people charge less than you would, then it doesn't mean you should drop your rate. And you certainly shouldn't be the one in the position of charging less – that's how the economy works. If you start charging less, you contribute to bringing the whole sector down. You're doing no one any favours by doing that.

Know your outgoings

As I mentioned earlier, when I first start mentoring a new client or business owner, the first question I ask is, *'What do you need to earn every month?'*

You have to know what you need to earn before you can even consider looking at what you'll charge. So, take a look at all your outgoings, and consider which ones – at least at this stage – aren't exactly luxuries.

Money Mindset

Money (it) Matters

~

There's a lot in the Pricing and Charging chapter of this book around the pitfalls that many small business owners fall into when trying to build their business and get more clients. It's okay, we all do it – we're not born business owners. Many of us have come from the corporate world having worked in just a small section of that company, with no real need for much thought about profit and loss. But, now it's real. Now it affects you.

We need money to survive – you have no employer safety net.

You're still a good person, but this is now serious. Stop trying to save the world and making sure everyone else is happy – make sure *you're* safe, first.

I know you could probably recite this list if you were asked, but sometimes, we all need a little reminder:

- You don't get sick pay

- You don't have someone else popping a few quid into your pension

- You don't have an endless supply of post-it notes and printer cartridges that Janet in Admin orders on your behalf

- You don't have holiday pay

- You don't have someone else magically putting milk into the fridge or bringing out sandwiches after board meetings

- You don't get paid for being late back from lunch

- You don't get paid for texting whilst on the toilet

- You don't get paid for being stuck in traffic

- You don't have an HR department that will smooth over that huge mistake you made and cost the company money

- You don't have a marketing and social media department (who are all really annoying on their bean bags but still actually really important in promoting your business)

It's just you, now – and you only have 24 hours in a day. I really suggest you eat and sleep for a few of those hours, too! So, if you're constantly 'giving back' or giving your time for free, or undercharging, or giving discounts, you're actually doing yourself more harm than the good you feel you're giving to others. Give back when you are creating enough income and profit. Make that a future goal. But not one for now.

Investment

As a business owner, there are things you're going to need to invest in, like insurance, technology, relevant registrations, mentors, etc., but there are things you don't need to think about, either – at least until you are making a profit.

A few weeks before writing this chapter, a client said to me, *'I'm going to write an online course, so shall I use (name of software withheld) – it's £199 a month?'*

I had a few questions to ask before I committed to a yes or a no, and I started with this one:

'How big is your audience?'

The answer? *'I don't really have one at the moment.'*

My line of enquiry finished there.

With no real audience, it's going to take a while to sell even a handful of copies of the course, so the investment in this all-singing all-dancing software which costs around £199 a month (yes – a month!) is going to be what I call negative expense. If my client was going to sell around 10 copies of the course every month for £20 then she'll be in profit by £1 each time. Oh, and that's without accounting for her time spent creating the course, marketing it, dealing with customer enquiries, etc.

Anyway, the answer was... No, just make the course a PDF download that gets delivered to customers via email. That's then all free for you and you can invest in the sparkly software when you are getting an income from sales that comfortably exceeds the software costs.

Software is one of the biggest unnecessary expenses for business owners. Using myself as an example, I use Zoom for my calls and webinars – and I pay for it. I need to pay for it, as I host webinars and meetings for large groups and regularly hold Power Hours. The cost of the software pays for itself given how many clients I have and how much I charge them, but if that all changed, I'd downgrade to the free plan until I needed the paid one again.

There is not one piece of software you absolutely need in order to make your business more successful. There's always a cheaper (or free) option.

Shiny object syndrome

There is no one item that you can buy that will turn your business into a six-figure business. That's achieved through a culmination of things, so stop buying everything that you see others buying until you know specifically how it will help you clear the things on your to-do list that get you closer to achieving a safe, sustainable and profitable business.

That course on how to get more likes on Instagram. Is it really necessary for you to buy it, even if it is only £15? Every penny counts. And you may not even need Instagram for your business – have you thought about that?

This is another example of why we looked at our hourly rate. If you buy that course for £15, then take the time to do the course and implement it, how long do you have to do paid work for in order to recoup that cost?

I'm not here to tell you you're rubbish with money. I'm just here to help you stay focused on the main reason I wrote this book; to help you create a safe, sustainable and profitable business that gives you money in the bank.

Clear that overdraft

Speak to your mortgage provider and your utility suppliers. Is there any movement or holiday on bills for a period of time until you get your overdraft straight?

Reduce your outgoings

Everyone can do this. The family might have to make some short-term sacrifices for your business, but I am sure you've made loads for them along the way, too.

Guilt

'I feel guilty charging full rate to mates.'

Well, that's why they come to you – because you're cheaper. But who's that helping? You've got to work more hours to recoup the lost money. That's a nice friendship, isn't it? Mates rates need to go, and anyone who asks has got a cheek!

'But they're a charity.'

I'm not sure where this *'I need to do it cheaper for charities'* thing comes from? When I was employed, I worked for one of England's longest running and biggest charities. Charities allocate money for services they need when they decide they need them. I have done work for charities as a self-employed business owner, but have never reduced my rate. They have funds. Chances are, it's the work you can provide for them that will help them increase those funds!

Realise your own worth – and others will do the same

I've only had it twice, but... hagglers! People who can't or don't want to pay full price but can *'offer exposure'* in return.

> *'I've already had three quotes at £9, £10 and £12 respectively because the work is quite straightforward and I will provide clear guidance.'*
>
> – (name withheld)

I don't care if the work can be done with my eyes closed – my rate is still my rate. You can't do it – but I can.

If someone has a job they can't – or don't want to – do themselves, then they're going to need someone who *does* want to do it; someone with experience and someone who cares about doing a good job. For that, they have to pay.

I appreciate places like Upwork and Fiverr etc., charge very little for tasks to be completed, but they're largely done by people whose cost of living is a lot less than those of us in developed countries, or who are employed elsewhere, or are teenagers/university students making some money on the side! They are not UK based business owners paying tax, NI and a mortgage! If a client wants to go there – let them.

Set your rates and remember you're not a market trader, so any haggling is met with a simple, 'No'.

Should I display my rates on my website?

Without a doubt – yes (as mentioned in the Foundations chapter). It makes things clear for people, and it also makes it difficult for them to haggle. It also shows confidence in your offering.

But let's look at some of the reasons why people don't put their rates on their website:

They're worried it will put people off.

Tough. Your prices are your prices. Having them on your website allows people to make a decision there and then without wasting their time – or indeed yours – in a lengthy awkward phone call or email chain. Imagine having to call a company you're really keen to work with, but then whilst on the phone with them you realise it's way out of your budget and now you need an awkward conversation to try and end the call. You don't want to put people in that position, and as I said, you don't need your time wasted, either.

They're not confident with what they charge.

Awkward! If you're not confident on your rate, then people will pick up on that and start haggling – successfully. Your rate is what you're worth, regardless of how long you've been in business.

They're hoping people will phone or email and then they can be converted to be a client.

Would you want to have to endure a sales pitch if you called someone just to find out their price? If someone can't afford you, there's very little anyone can do to magic up the money, so save your time for those who can afford what you're worth.

Their prices are not that straightforward.

Why not? How about sorting out some packages of your most popular or bestselling services, as I mentioned in the Foundations chapter? Pop them on your website with easy to follow pricing, making it as clear as possible for people to know what they're getting.

Dave down the chippy told me not to share my prices.

Please, Dave – do tell?

Consider this. If your competitors have their prices on their website, where are potential clients more likely to go in search of an easy solution?

Be more virtual

Meetings and Travel: Can your meeting be done by video conference? Do you really need to be there in person? The person you're meeting might prefer a call! They've got work to do, too! Consider a conference call and 'sell it' to your client as you simply valuing their time.

Always consider what something is 'actually' costing you before signing on the dotted line. Take some time to know something's worth. As well as your own.

Niche and Ideal Client Avatars

'He could sell ice to an eskimo'

Well that's cool, but why even try? Sell it to the new cocktail bar that's opened in town

~

We've all had this conversation:

'I'm struggling to get clients'

'Oh, okay... what's your niche? You've got a niche, right? You need a niche!'

Yeah, thanks for that, but what's a niche? And why, pray tell, do I need one?

A niche is an area of expertise or a specific group of people/clients you cater for. Want the dictionary definition?

Niche: Relating to products, services or interests that appeal to a small and specialised section of the population.

For example, if you're a wedding planner, your niche is 'wedding planning' and your demographic is 'couples planning on getting married'.

You can't just think 'well, everyone can buy my stuff', because not everyone *needs* that stuff, do they?

In addition to niche, there are many people who say that in order to have a successful business you need to define your 'ideal client avatar' (ICA), which in a nutshell, means you need to know who you're selling to. In my wedding planner example, that's exactly what's needed. A wedding planner isn't going to be targeting those who are looking to get divorced, are they?

However, the purpose of finding your ICA has become lost, exaggerated, mis-informed and over-complicated over time; mainly by people who spout loads of advice in theory but in reality are just playing fast and loose with an *actual* expert's solid advice. Trying to make it look like a new idea, most probably.

You'd have heard or read about people identifying their ICA (wow, that phrase actually makes me feel bilious) and telling you that you can't possibly hope to sell anything or get clients until you've nailed it. They say there's no way you can know how to word your marketing and sales pitches until you know exactly what your potential client eats, at what time of the day they start digesting it, and which hand they wipe their... mouth with afterwards.

Such is the pressure of this 'advice', that some people focus so heavily on identifying their ICA, it actually stops them from ever progressing in their business. They stop marketing because they worry they're not speaking to the *right* people, and some of them decide they probably need to re-brand their whole offer to suit. Hell, some of them give up entirely and sod off travelling for a year until they 'get clear' on their ICA. It's become so disjointed and confusing that many business owners think they can't move on until they know exactly who they are talking to. Talk about stereotyping!

I've seen many a person come up all proud with their ICA, even down to the types of shoes they wear (because they've been told they need to know this stuff). Yes, really.

If defining the shoes someone might wear works for you, and you're making the profit in your business that you want to make, *and* your business is following my 20% Rule®, *and* you're not struggling with consistent content or regular leads, then brilliant! But what happens if you find out your ideal client actually wears Skechers and wouldn't be seen dead in the pair of Converse you'd lovingly noted on your ICA picture-thing?

I'm not dismissing the idea of an ICA completely (especially if you're reading this and you're a shoe salesperson), but I need to explain why I have a different take on identifying your niche, and why your 'ideal client' focus may actually be stopping you from getting leads from a nice and diverse range of people and places.

Ideal client avatar. Such a buzzword, though.

Purpose of a niche

Remember; niche relates to products, services or interests that appeal to a small and specialised section of the population. So, a niche is something you specialise in doing, providing or selling. It's not about identifying who you'd quite fancy working with – because those people might not want or need your services!

Aha! See?

The purpose of your niche is to help you market what you offer to people who need it.

You may well want to work with 'heart-centred female leaders', but what if those female leaders don't need what you're selling?

Throughout this book, you'll notice I like to use various real-life analogies. I find that these help to explain key business messages. I feel like I can talk from a place of experience because each of these things

I've actually gone through or witnessed myself as a small business owner (and mentor).

Let's have a another of my own examples of niche for good measure, shall we?

There's a service provider on LinkedIn (other platforms are available) who has a real love of cats. I know this because her business tagline states that fact, and much of her marketing talks about felines and the funny furry foibles they have. But, her services have absolutely nothing to do with cats. Likewise, her services aren't very likely going to be of any use to cats, either – just in case that was her thinking. Based on her service, her audience is going to be small business owners. Yes, she may well attract people who also like cats (likeminded people, etc.), but she's forgetting one fundamental thing about marketing: She's not telling people what she actually does. She doesn't mention what problems she solves or why people might need her services. And, because she never tells anyone, the cat loving audience aren't following her for the right reasons. They're not going to give, win or bring her any business. She's built up a relationship around cats, and not what she sells. This is going to throw people a hairball. I mean, curveball.

The only reason I personally know what she does is because I found the constant cat-related content a bit odd and became curious (make your own jokes, please). I was thinking that she was maybe some sort of cat whisperer...

She's not.

Her 'ideal client' of cat lovers may not need what she's selling! You heard it here first.

So, whilst it's true that we do tend to be attracted to people who are like us and like what we like, it doesn't mean we're going to automatically want to work with them (or them with us), because they may not need what we're selling! So, if you're spending far too much time, money and energy on your 'ideal' people to work with, you're missing the point of your marketing:

To tell people what you sell.

Drop the ICA

Wait, I invested so much time in defining my ideal client avatar, I am NOT ditching it!

If you're getting consistent leads from those people, fine. Definitely don't ditch. Ignore this section.

Wait. You're *not?* Best keep reading, then.

Now, just because someone says you need an ICA, it doesn't make having one that secret ingredient to being able to run every department in your business, turn a healthy profit, and achieve a holiday home in North Wales. There's so much more you have to think about when it comes to niche.

Over recent years, there has been a massive influx of female coaches into the world of business. As a result, the number of people targeting female coaches as their ICA has massively increased, too. Check out the headlines on LinkedIn if you don't believe me!

Let's say you really want to work with female coaches (because you've been told to have an ICA), and your service is all about 'money mindset', for example.

What if female coaches don't want to know about money mindset, and none of them take you up on your offer?

What if your style, your content, or your overall vibe just doesn't click with female coaches, and they actively gravitate away from you?

What if you work with a couple of female coaches, but you find out they're really bad payers and cause you all sorts of planning problems?

Are you still going to continue targeting only female coaches, because someone who makes money out of selling the business dream tells you that you have to focus on one type of person? Had you not been so specific in the 'who', then you could have spent more time showcasing the 'what' – and therefore attracting people who really do want to work with you.

Wait – I know, if you really bought into the ICA thing elsewhere, then you'll have your hand up right now and will be wanting to tell me that *'we can't appeal to everybody'*. You're right – we can't. Just look at Brexit! Actually, don't. My point is, there will always be a divide – but perhaps let people make that decision about you and your business themselves, before you decide you're not even going to give them the option of working with you.

Trust me, your messaging, your tone of voice, and your actual services **will** attract paying clients who want – and need – to work with you; without you needing to know the patterns of their digestive cycle.

'Whilst I was sitting in bed this morning, thinking, 'do I need the toilet or not', I thought, 'goodness, I am so regular, it's always at 6am'. Do you have regular bowel movements at 6am, too? If so, buy my marketing communications mentorship package for just £695, now!'

Ridiculous.

As proof of practicing what I preach, I currently don't have an ICA. Other than the fact that they need to be able to pay me, obviously.

I don't envisage any one particular person when writing my content. Nobody at all. I simply think about the message I want to get across, the conversation I want to start, and the questions I'd like opinions on.

I must stress in fairness that people who have an ICA don't necessarily fail in business, but they also don't always nail it either. They're stuck; focused on one area. They're stuck on who they want to work with, and often forget to listen to their audience. They essentially cut out people who may genuinely want to work with them.

Forget the who and concentrate on the what.

Then, tell people all about it!

Stop being just about 'who you serve'

Let's go back to our wedding planner analogy. Yes, if you're a wedding planner, you need to be talking to people who are newly engaged or planning a wedding etc., but it doesn't stop there. You also need to be talking about what it is you can do for those people. Just because they're captive, doesn't mean they'll willingly pay if you're not offering what they want or need. Wedding planning is hugely diverse. Do you cater for weddings abroad as well as at home? Do you do all the admin? Do you turn up on the day to support? Your clients – and indeed people in general – need to know this stuff. So, tell them.

We all know that one of the best ways we can get extra work is if other people talk about us positively, but we need them to be talking about *what* we do as well as how great we are. Encourage your clients to do this when they give you testimonials.

Forget a sector niche

As a Business Mentor, I regularly get enquiries from people who are looking to better their life and start their own service-based business for the first time. They've downloaded all the free stuff and read all the free advice online, yet many are hit by that brick wall of niching and thinking that you can't possibly get a client until you define it.

Again, as with ICAs, this is rubbish.

You can still stand out and attract clients without a niche. Really.

I had an enquiry via Instagram from a lady who was interested in starting her own admin service business. She'd already digested everything there was to know about the need for an ICA and a niche and had come up with the solution of catering to 'carers'. She wanted to provide admin support to carers. Somewhere, some marketing guru was delighted with that headline.

Intrigued by the niching, I asked more questions.

This lady had years of experience working in the care industry and the NHS. She'd worked efficiently and effectively at putting rotas together for district nurses and carers who went out into the community 24/7.

Here was my first problem… what admin support do district nurses and carers require that they do themselves and would therefore benefit from outsourcing?

The answer? Nothing. Someone at the hospital or clinic (such as my lady in her previous role) would do it all for them.

Can you see how niching and essentially targeting a market that can give her no business very nearly put this lady *out* of business before she'd even started?

We also discussed the fact that carers are notoriously underpaid, and so even if there was a sector whereby they could choose to outsource some of their expected tasks to someone else, chances are they'd be invoiced to the tune of double their own hourly rate. The whole model was just plain wrong – even though on paper it ticked all the niching boxes.

There's no denying that this lady had amazing and truly invaluable skills to offer, but the marketing advice of niching to a certain sector or client base was totally unrealistic and doomed to fail.

Let's look at this lady's skills and see if we can give her some better opportunities and marketing advice, shall we? She can easily put together rotas for different shift patterns, and she's got a track record of organising people in a massive organisation here, there and everywhere. She could sell her services to a whole range of businesses who could benefit from those skills. I'm thinking she could happily provide services to business owners who have a busy itinerary of travel, or business owners who are based in various locations around the world, or perhaps even parents whose children are schooled in a different country and need to coordinate flights home. One specific skill set – many different sectors to attract.

Those types of clients are also more likely to have the money to invest, so if you really must niche, at least go where the money is! It's not all about money, of course, but this whole book is about creating a business model that gives you a profit, after all!

Limiting yourself to a sector or person means you're limited not only because those people may not want, need or be able to afford your service, but also because that sector could easily go under. Look at everything that's happened with COVID-19. Look at how many industries literally stopped in their tracks (or even threw themselves on them).

Remember that this book wants you to look at making your business safe and sustainable as well as bringing you a profit, so please remember that if who you're providing services for goes under... YOU go under, too.

Make your niche your services

I do have something to say about niching. You can go ahead and niche your services.

See? I'm not totally disregarding the word!

Choose those services that you can offer and that you hopefully love doing. That's your niche.

Talk about what services you provide, what problems they solve, and why people should be choosing to invest in them. The enquiries will come so much faster than if you're talking about who you want to work with.

One of my own services as a VA is email marketing, so I promote that as a niche to attract people who specifically want or need help in that area. I enjoy it, I know how to do it well, and I get good results. So, that's my niche – or one of them anyway. I really don't like limiting myself to one thing!

Remember that I don't then limit that service to a specific client. I'll work with anyone if they meet a few criteria:

- They are organised (someone with no real plan drives me insane)

- They are unlikely to say, *'Oh, but my mate Dave down the chippy reckons if you put this in your newsletter everyone will open it'*. (Er, I'm the professional, thanks)

- They won't claim to have not received my invoice (payment is essential, always)

Create your own criteria. You'll find you'll be much happier about your working.

It took me 12 months, but I realised that in having one main niche in my services meant that my marketing got a hell of a lot easier. You can always change that niche later on, but for now, sell what you love doing.

Make it easy for people to spend money with you.

Marketing and Messaging

You're only human – as are your potential clients

~

My marketing and messaging tips are based around modern methods; social media, website content and blogging. That's where the world is right now.

If you want advice on the face to face marketing stuff, this book isn't going to give you it, I'm afraid. I personally hate networking.

Let's move on before I rant.

So, as you may already know, the concept of *know, like and trust* underpins all of your marketing. You need to allow people to get to know, like and trust you in order for them to feel comfortable investing in you. There will always be some people who buy from you on a whim, of course, but the majority of your clients will invest in you when they've ticked off one, two or all three of those factors.

But, in a world that's largely virtual, how do we get people to feel like they know, like and can trust you without even having met you?

The first thing you need to do is remember that there is no business owner on this earth who can attract everyone and appeal to them all. There is always opinion. Don't try to please. It'll slow you down.

Become the expert

We need you to become known as the expert in your field. So, when someone says, *'I am looking for someone who is/can do XYZ'*, we want people to say your name in response.

This is why your messaging has to centre around *what* you do – not *who* you do it for.

That's what we use our blogs, website content and social media presence for.

Write content that others want to read

I used to put out a lot of content about how if someone invested in my services they'd have more time for that longed-for work-life balance everyone goes on about, until one day, someone commented and said, *'If I had you working with me, I wouldn't use the extra time I gained for any work-life balance nonsense, I'm more interested in spending that extra time in my business!'*

It was a good point! Not everyone wants time freed-up to galivant across fields with daisies in their hair! Some people want to get stuck in with building their empire.

After this one encounter and realisation, I suddenly had this ability to think up extra content. I now talked about how my services could free people up to work in – and on – their businesses. I started to attract more clients because of it, because my messaging attracted a wider audience of people. Simple.

For example, when I was new in business and was in a membership group with other service-based business owners, one member asked the group, *'How does everyone organise their electronic files?'* I initially rolled my eyes because I thought the answer was obvious, until a load more members started commenting that it was a good question and that they'd often wondered about the answer themselves. So, I used the inspiration to write a blog post entitled, *'How to Organise Electronic Files'.* I put it together in ten minutes and immediately popped a link to it in the comments of the original post. Greetings, from Catherine the Established Expert on Electronic File Storage.

Yes, it got me some clients. Why? Because I'd solved a problem and shown myself to be the expert.

Ask yourself this:

What pain points do your services address or resolve for your clients?

Think of five of them.

Now you have ideas for five pieces of content that are going to establish you as the expert. Go, you!

How to attract potential clients

Draw people to you by giving them what they want and what they need. Resonate with them through your messaging.

Imagine phoning a friend and inviting them out to dinner. She's got a shellfish allergy, so you're not going to put forward the new seafood restaurant as an option, are you? Pitch your content in a way that makes your potential clients think, *'They understand me / they know what I need / they know what they're on about / they're an expert'*.

Here are a couple of examples of my own pieces of content (titles):

- How to delegate better: a guide for small business owners

- Reduce the risk of errors in your bookkeeping

- Top tips for healthy small business bookkeeping

- How to get your first 1000 email subscribers

Each piece is based around the services I offer. They address and solve the pain points my clients have, and therefore show me as an expert – someone they can trust.

One thing that Brand Strategist, Phil Pallen, asks his clients is, '*Who are you and why should I care?*' I love this. He's right. Why should anyone care what you're saying?

Here are a couple of examples of addressing that issue:

> *Post 1: I'm writing my second book to help your business be safe, sustainable and profitable. Pre-order a copy here...*

> *Post 2: My next book? It's to help business owners ensure their business is safe, sustainable and profitable. I'm writing it after having to urgently take time out of my own business for four months (brain surgery), yet suffering no loss of income, because I'd always prepared for such eventualities. I don't preach and I don't judge. I just share what works for me and how it can work for you, too.*

> *Why?*

> *Because we all deserve a happy, healthy, stress-free working life.*

> *Find out more here...*

I put both of these posts out on the same day / same time in different weeks, to test them for the purpose of proving something in this book. I sold copies from the second post. Nothing from the first. You can see why, can't you?

Going back to Phil's comment; '*Who are you and why should I care?*'

Because, what you're offering could change their life, that's why.

It's not about you

Think about all those posts you've seen that start with things like this:

> '*I love it when a client recommends me...*'

> '*We've just won...*'

'I've been nominated...'

They're all about the writer.

How about we change them a little, yes?

> *'Claire, thank you so much for your recent recommendation...'* (tag in Claire – great for both of your reaches and profiles).
>
> *'Thank you so much to everyone who voted for us...'*
>
> *'I've nominated myself for an award...'* (I actually shared this post once and it got so much attention because it made people laugh and it resonated with so many people. We all know most people who've 'been' nominated have done it themselves!)

Make your posts fun, engaging, salesy on occasion, educational or personal. Make them resonate with people.

Don't ever miss out the sales posts, otherwise you might as well miss out all of them.

Consistency is key. You don't have to post all day every day (quality over quantity, please), but you do need to spend time every single day thinking about your marketing.

Fun, hey?

What to say

Be helpful, solve problems, build relationships.

Give people value in the form of tips and ideas. Quit with the bombardment of memes and motivational quotes, unless that's what you're selling. Remember the cat lady from the previous chapter? Her cute cat pics will get her so far, but it won't generate income, and this means your business is not safe, sustainable and/or profitable. Content for content's sake is a no-no.

Talk about what problems you're solving – and talk about how you've already solved someone's problem and how it's made their life wonderful as a result. You may need to make money from this, but you're only going to do it if you can understand your clients' needs in going about it.

People don't like to be sold, but they love to buy.

– Jeffrey Gitomer

When I first started working with my own Virtual Assistant, it enabled me to really understand what it's like for business owners to hand over their business to someone else for the first time – and really emphasised the need to allow people to get to know, like and trust you first.

I had a fair idea of how it felt for my clients, as my own business had always been so very important to me. The thought of handing that over to someone else and potentially putting my reputation on the line was scary. But it wasn't until I did it for real that I got an insight.

So, here are some things to think about – and some questions to answer in your marketing.

- How do your clients feel when they first start working with you?

- What do your potential clients feel when they get in touch?

- How do those who haven't yet got in touch feel about working with you?

- What stops someone getting in touch when they first find out about you?

Ease people's fears and break down those barriers!

Engage

If you have a day when you really have nothing to say on your own feed, comment on the posts of others.

When I mentor someone who's social media activity is zero, I recommend they start by spending 20 minutes a day scrolling and commenting – on the best platforms we've identified for their business (in other words, where their clients are likely to be).

I recommend they do this twice a day, every day! I say twice a day so that if they've replied to one comment in the morning, they can go back later and see the results.

You can do this from your bed in the morning and at night! There are no excuses not to. You can always find something to comment on and add value. Don't leave it days before you reply to a comment or question, though, because conversations move on quickly. Likewise, though, you don't have to reply within mere minutes!

Find posts that interest you – they don't have to be business related. Those non-business posts allow people to get to know you! I once got repeat business after commenting on a very busy post about my favourite curry dish! Hot leads indeed!

Once you're confident in the art of engagement, start putting out some content of your own.

Now, let's be realistic. It's hard to get people to engage with your stuff, and sometimes you can put out a post and nobody comments or even likes it. I do remember those early days, and I still get posts that get little or no interaction every so often. I remember the first time, thinking, will anyone ever like any of my posts? It takes time and consistency, though. Business needs to be attracted – people aren't searching for you if they don't know you exist!

So, what should you do if you're getting no engagement and no traction?

Delete it? Stop doing social media altogether? Shut down your business?

No, no, no. None of the above!

If nobody has commented or liked the post, what's the point in deleting it? To save face? To save embarrassment? Who from, if nobody has seen it?

Ah, see! You know people have seen it, don't you!

Look, do you like or comment on every post you see when you're out there scrolling? I'm going to guess the answer is no. Who has that kind of time? I can guarantee that people are seeing your post, despite what the stats might tell you on some social media platforms. I've had a 'Reach of 0' and 21 comments before, so their maths is questionable, at best.

Look, any content that is relevant to your business is worthy of staying there, it also helps people get to know, like and trust you, and shows your business is open and thinking about providing! You're creating authority and showing you're around for a long time. If you keep deleting posts that don't get as many comments or likes that you think you need, then you'll have no content out there and people will think you're either not trading or simply have nothing to offer. Massive waste of time to delete.

What would you think if you went to check out someone's social media profile and they either hadn't posted for months, or hadn't posted ever? You'd be wary, I'm sure.

Keep going! As I said, not everybody likes and comments on every post they see. I certainly don't, and it's in some people's nature never to do it at all. Don't be disheartened if you're getting no engagement initially. People need to get to know you and that takes time. You don't go up to strangers in the street and start talking to them about your business and then say, *'So, you gunna buy from me or what?'*

I hope you don't, at least.

Here are some stumbling blocks people usually throw in their own way when it comes to posting or sharing content:

'I don't know the etiquette'

What etiquette? You can even swear on social media these days! Gasp! Well, it helps attract people who don't mind swearing – and gets rid of those in your audience who do! Those that might be offended by a swear word would not make a good client if they then go on to find out in real life that you swear, too. You'd have to constantly watch your Ps and Qs and that's no fun. Be you! Trying to be anything else is just exhausting and attracts people who don't get the real you – and they'll be an absolute nightmare to work with. People who are just like you make the best clients, so speak in the way you'd speak to yourself.

'I don't know what I'm doing!'

We learn by mimicking others and by observing what's going on around us, which is why I suggested starting off by exploring, reading and commenting on other people's posts. Have a read of the other comments, whilst you're there. You'll see what works and you'll find your flow when it comes to creating your own content.

Now, if you've been using social media consistently for many years and you're still not getting any engagement, you're doing something wrong, so here's how to turn that around:

Check who you're following and/or connected with. Now is the time to check you've ditched the ICA restrictions. Expand your connections, expand who you're following, expand your own audience and remember, you never know who knows who – or what they're doing on the side that might warrant your involvement.

Ask questions and share content to entice people to comment and engage. This is easy to do when you think about what kinds of things make *you* comment.

- Evoke an emotion or some kind of nostalgia

- Discuss something of interest to you personally (or professionally)

- Encourage people to talk about themselves

Please don't post stuff like, '*What are you doing this weekend – pop a gif in the comments!*' because busy people haven't got time to be doing things like that, and busy people are the ones you want to get the attention of. Why? Because if they're busy, they have an income.

Ask questions that are relevant to you but also relevant to them. Show your personality, too – and don't overthink it. Just be you.

I have some great tips for all of this on my YouTube channel. There's a link over on my website catherinegladwyn.co.uk

Being you

Now's the time to show people you're investable, you're likeable, and you're an expert.

You may not be all of these things to all people, but there's someone for everyone, and that means there are clients out there for you! Some people will go as far as to love you, and when your stuff resonates with them, they'll realise they need what you offer.

Ditch the imposter syndrome because it's going to hold you back. You're your own worst enemy if you don't keep telling people who you are and what you can do for them. If you suffer a touch of imposter syndrome, just remember why you set up in business in the first place. You know you're good at what you do.

Think about some of the people that you follow on social media. Think about who you've bought from in the past and think about why you did it. Is it because they showed they live a lifestyle you want? Is it because they were honest about the way they parent their kids? Is it because you admired something they do for charity? Something attracted you and made you choose them. Now you have to figure out what's going to draw people to you in the same way.

Share enough to show your values, but not enough to show you're not focused. For example, share stories about your kids to show the kind of person you are, but don't give enough detail that suggests you don't actually have enough time or focus for your work. Make sense? Some days I don't get dressed because I suffer with fatigue as part of my Addison's Disease, and I won't jump in the shower until perhaps 4pm so that my energy can be used on running my business and meeting my clients' needs and expectations. Even though that would resonate with many people, I don't share it with my audience because many people don't understand fatigue. They think it's something you can get rid of with a twenty-minute nap at lunchtime. I don't ever want people to think I am lazy – that's one thing I'm really not – and I don't want to get into an argument with ignorant people, so I just don't use it in my marketing!

Easier read than done? It takes time, granted, and you're not going to get a conversation going after 'a few weeks of really focusing on social media'.

Imagine you're in a ridiculously crowded room and everyone's been there for an hour already. You stand at the door and start talking. Why would people want to stop their already flowing conversations and start listening to you? It'll take time and consistency. People need to hear you, see you, and get familiar with you. They need to know you've not just crashed the wrong party. Be consistent but remember that this word does not mean you have to post 24/7.

Worried about getting things wrong with spelling and stuff? Don't be. Perfection in your posts isn't necessary, really! Since my last tumour, I have genuinely lost the ability to put commas in the right place, and my decades of ridiculing one of my long-term friends on his inability to use the correct there/their/they're has come back and bitten me on the backside, as I've now lost that, too.

Allow any fear to drive you. Push through it and break that comfort zone.

You're only human, as are your potential clients!

Say it again

You don't always have to be creating new content. You can repurpose content again and again, or simply rewrite something to update or refresh it.

Sadly, not everybody will see something you posted the first time. Or if they did, they may well go on to forget all about it. If a post does well, share it again in the future and give it a shot at a new audience. You could even do it with a post that got nothing the first time around, actually. Give it a try.

In the case of a blog, think about *how* you're sharing your content. For example, if you're a sleep coach for tired business owners and you've written a great blog on how to tackle those 4am wake-ups, how would you introduce that info to your audience?

'Read my blog about sleeping' (link to blog)

I'm going to think, 'why'? I'm busy, and I have no idea what you're going to tell me.

So how about this, then:

'Tired of waking up at 4am and thinking about your business? Here are four things you can quickly implement to help eradicate what's stopping you from getting a full night's sleep' (link to blog)

Much more focused. I know which one I'd click.

Here's another example. Let's say you're a time management expert:

'Read my blog about being productive' (link to blog)

Again, why would I click? Plus, if my time management is poor, should I really be reading a blog?

How about this:

'Need help with your time management? Here are four easy to implement things you can do right now in my 3-minute blog' (link to blog)

Which one would you stop scrolling for and click on?

Call to action

Blogs, social media content and your website. They all need a call to action (CTA) of some sort.

Here are some things you could round off your pieces of content with:

- Sign up to my newsletter…

- If you'd like to guest blog for me on the following subjects, get in touch…

- Ready to work with me? Here's how…

- Let's connect… (social media icons)

- Here's a link to the services I've mentioned…

- Read my other blog on this subject here…

Even non-sales posts on social media benefit from having a call to action, even if it's just a question to get people talking and keep the conversation (and engagement) going.

How do I know what's working?

When people contact you, ask them where they found you. Don't be alarmed when the reply starts with, *'Actually, I've been stalking you for a while on social media….'*

Make sure you ask people this question personally. Avoid sending them a survey or giving them a list on a dropdown menu on your contact form. People are time poor so will often select the first option, or not really think about their response because they'll view it as a tick-box exercise. But, if you ask them personally, whether that's on a conference call or face to face, you're more likely to get a considered, accurate response – that may just surprise you.

Lead magnets

What are lead magnets?

Magnets that lead people to your paid-for services – simple.

Savvy business owners often give away small bits of knowledge and info in their service area so that people can see that they're the expert and thus get to know, like and trust them in the process.

Lead magnets are bits of advice – top tips, 'how to' guides, etc., – that people download in exchange for their email address. This is a great currency for you to have, by the way.

Free stuff

I detest the notion that you have to give away loads of stuff for free in order to get people to buy from you. What usually happens if you give lots away for free is that you largely attract freeloaders, or you spend so much time giving that you run out of time to earn.

That free Facebook group you started as a lead magnet that doesn't convert – now you've considered your hourly rate and how much time you spend in there, ditch it. Close it.

That lead magnet that never does its job in leading to anyone ever buying anything from you. Rewrite it and consider taking stuff out – are you giving people so much help in it that they don't actually need you for anything else?

People who don't see the value in your services and people who download and sign up for every latest shiny thing and do nothing with it are largely time wasters. But, you will sometimes attract people who want to get to know you more and who do soak it up. They may well convert to paying clients, but is the ROI worth it?

It's often a small number that converts well from lead magnets and free stuff, so you really shouldn't be spending too much time creating these things. It may not earn you anything, so make sure you don't lose out, either.

Content

Who else had a Rubik's cube in the 80s?

~

What is content?

Your content includes things like your blog, web pages, PR, testimonials, case studies and your social media posts.

By sharing your content over and over again, you can reach a larger and newer audience – and give a reminder to those who saw it the first time about how great you are and what you can do for them.

Sharing content specifically on social media comes under the heading of 'content marketing'.

What is content marketing?

'Content marketing is a marketing technique of creating and distributing valuable, relevant and consistent content to attract and acquire a clearly defined audience – with the objective of driving profitable customer action'.

– Forbes, 2014

It's basically anything you write and send out there to the world either physically or online, so from leaflets to LinkedIn… and everything in between.

Engagement

What do we want? *Engagement!*

When do we want it? *As often as possible!*

Cheery as this is, you're not going to get it all the time (sadly).

Not all posts on social media will get a response, but that doesn't mean they're rubbish or not working. Sales posts, for example, rarely get any engagement. I mean, come on... do you ever really comment on a post to say *'bought that!'* or *'buying that!'* every time you see the advert?

We looked briefly at how to change some social media posts in the Marketing and Messaging chapter, so that you can get more interaction on them. I've shared those again here (yay for repurposing), but I've also thrown in some extras and set you some tasks to implement as well.

So:

> *'Read my blog about sleeping' (link to blog)*

Becomes...

> *'Tired of waking up at 4am and thinking about your business? Here are four things you can quickly implement to help eradicate what's stopping you from getting a full night's sleep' (link to blog)*

And another one:

> *'Read my blog about being productive' (link to blog)*

Becomes...

> *'Need help with your time management? Here are four easy to implement things you can do right now in my 3-minute blog' (link to blog)*

Which ones would you stop scrolling for and click on?

Now – imagine this! You've just found a Rubik's cube whilst tidying out the loft. You loved this colourful cube of delight as a kid. Let's talk about that with your audience!

Which works best for engagement do you think – and why?

1. *'I just found a Rubik's cube in my loft. I loved these as a kid'*

2. *'Who else had a Rubik's cube in the 80s? I think my best time was 4 weeks and 13 days, and that included peeling the stickers off. What about you?'*

I'm hoping you chose number two. Number one is a statement and all about you. It doesn't really give people a place to 'go'. It might get some comments from people who say, *'I loved them, too'* and you'll reply with *'great'* and then that's it. But the second one gets a proper conversation going and gives people an insight into your personality – know, like and trust, remember.

The second one actively invites people to comment and to talk about themselves. This makes people feel comfortable. People generally like that.

Dealing with negativity

What I have found with negative comments on my content is that it's always about one or two specific things – the person themselves, or money. Sometimes both.

Since starting my business, I've had endless support from all those around me – family, friends and ex-colleagues. They all know I'm someone who sees through everything I say I'm going to do. Even the people I've met in business groups know I'm organised and will see through any plans to the end. I've watched those people do the same. I've learned from them and shared with them, and it's been a great part of my success being around others experiencing the same obstacles and wins.

Indeed, everything was fabulous. Until I announced I was writing my first book… *How to be a Virtual Assistant*.

Oh, the comments.

Nobody specifically said, '*You can't make this work*', but instead I found that I got kicked out of groups, blocked by page owners, and had ridiculous emojis added to my comments. I even noticed that I had the same people pop up on my Google analytics over and over again. People were even phoning my clients and trying to badmouth me. Fortunately, I follow my own advice when it comes to attracting the right clients, and so they all stood by me (ideal), but it didn't make me feel any better. Certainly not at first.

Where did this all stem from? Two witches (there's no nicer word to use, I'm afraid) thought my book sales would reduce the sales of their online courses.

They probably did, to be fair – but that's not my problem if they've become complacent in what they do!

Like I said earlier, negativity is usually about the person spreading it and / or money. This was one of those occasions where it was both.

I was initially surprised at grown adult business owners acting the way they were without contacting me directly, but I also found it quite energising and saw it as a green light saying, '*You can obviously do this because they're scared*'. It's sometimes hard to grasp, but we're not all chasing the same clients and we will never control the whole market. I've learnt this from huffing off from many a Monopoly game, believe me.

Obviously, my 'fans' were running scared, though. So, every time they (or anyone) said or did something particularly negative, I wrote another chapter of my book. They were my ignition.

I hope you'll take on board what I've said as a learning opportunity. If you receive any negativity, consider it a form of praise. They're telling you that you're a threat, you're not in their shadow, and you're about to take over because they've become complacent.

Remember when we talked about nobody seeing or engaging with our posts? If you're getting the negativity, you're being seen, trust me. You're getting known for what you do – and that's bloody amazing!

My first book has gone on to be a multi-award winning bestseller and was listed as one of ten best business books written by women in The Independent, so who has the right to leave one-finger emojis now?

Turn negativity into energy – and annoy your haters or doubters in the process. Remember that if they're absolutely nailing their business and winning at life, they wouldn't have time, energy or desire to attack you, now would they?

Keep sharing

Don't forget, just because you've shared something once does not mean that everyone saw it, and even if they did, they may well have forgotten the content – so remind them!

Do you get a reminder from your dentist? I do, and thank God, because I'd have no teeth left in my head if they didn't give me the same message more than once.

How often do you see the same adverts on the TV? Each one costs a lot of money to run, but they don't just show it once, do they? Companies pay for it to be shown countless times. They're not doing it to be annoying, they're trying to stay on your radar and they're trying to capture the attention of as many different people as possible. With social media, people are online at different times, on different days, and for different reasons – you'll never attract the attention of everyone in one go, so don't just share something once. It'll be a waste.

How often should you share?

It depends on how well the piece of content converts. If it's not seemingly doing much to get you leads or follow-ups then you might want to only share it once every three months, perhaps? If it's great at converting, though, you'll need to put it out there regularly, so perhaps once a month or once a fortnight as part of a bank of lots of other content to share around it.

I started promoting this book before I'd even written the first chapter. In fact, I hadn't even defined the tag line. My audience (maybe you) helped me with that – but as soon as it got close to me finishing every chapter, I was promoting the book every day. Yes – every day!

Keep things on people's radars.

Clickbait

You've heard of clickbait, right? It's not all about *'I can't believe this girl went from 300lbs to 130lbs by doing THIS at the Drive Thru McDonald's'*.

Clickbait is, again, about drawing the reader in so they'll follow a link.

For example, I have a lead magnet called (ironically), *'How to write newsletter subject headings that get opened'*. Just sharing the link won't grab much attention, so instead I draw people in, like this:

> *'Are you sending great newsletters but they're not even getting opened?*
>
> *Download my free tips on how to write newsletter subject headings that people want to click.'*

People are much more likely to click when they can immediately see something is of interest to them. Either way, it's going to be clicked much more than if I had just shared a generic-looking link and title.

Schedule

Don't worry, you don't need to trawl through your blog posts every day to see which one to post. Instead, schedule them. If that means it's time to invest in some scheduling software then it's worth it, as it means your business keeps getting noticed even when you're busy, on holiday, or when the cat's vomited on the laptop.

I use and recommend MeetEdgar, but there are many others out there. You could even share a subscription with another business owner – I do this with a couple of pieces of software. Sharing the cost is always a good thing, right?

Blog bank

I can almost guarantee this section of the book about blogging will be one that's overlooked, because EFFORT, right?

Tough!

Like I said, you're here for a reason and blogging needs to happen to get you where you need to be. I know how much many of you hate it, or spend too much time on it, or have never started, so I'm going to make it easy for you.

Blogging is important, and here are just five reasons why:

- They're great for Search Engine Optimisation (SEO – getting you up the ranks on Google)

- They provide you with a content bank

- They show your personality

- They demonstrate your expertise

- They get you known for what you do

When you start blogging, you will start with zero, obviously. I did! I didn't come into business with a bank of content and a bank of blogs, but now I have so many that I can't remember what I've written about. I don't reflect on my blogging and think 'OMG, *I remember each blog was such an effort and I nearly died whilst writing three of them*'.

It was only two.

When I first started blogging, after extensive research I found that the word count was recommended to be 350 to 550, and I've stuck with that, but there are varying reports on Google that say you should aim for more. Just get started; get writing. It's so much more about the content than the number of words.

Here are my tips to make blogging easier:

1. Speak it (I dictate my blogs into a transcription app. It's 90% perfect, sometimes more. I then just copy and paste it into my website. I can then blog in bed if I so wish, or whenever/wherever something comes to me)

2. Go for 350-550 words (don't aim for more if you really can't – life's too short)

3. Repurpose it (use snippets for other content, such as social media posts)

4. Answer frequently Googled questions (again, it's great for SEO)

5. Get other people to write them (I have a few blogs where I've started the intro and then asked others for their expert opinion as contributors. For example, while I was recovering from brain surgery (I make it sound so casual), I wrote an extremely popular and widely shared article on *'The best gifts to buy your clients this Christmas'*. But I actually didn't write any of it. The people who wanted to have their gifts included wrote a blurb, provided a photo and gave me the links to their website! I just pasted them in!)

Types of blogs to have:

1. Guest blogs from other people who enhance your field and widen your audience

2. Frequently Asked Questions (and answers, obviously)

3. Case Studies

4. Address pain points or misconceptions around your services

5. Why people need to work with you – what problems you solve

Google is the number one search engine (as you'll likely know), so you need to be coming up on it – and blogging can really help you with that.

Blog layout

The layout of your blog isn't overly important, but in my opinion must include these four elements – especially the last one!

- Entice

- Outline

- Teach / Advise

- Provide a Call to Action

Entice the reader so that they're encouraged (and want) to read on.

Outline what the blog will cover – you can do that in the title or within the opening paragraph.

Teach / advise the audience through what you promised in the title and or first paragraph. This is important for sharing your knowledge and showing your authority – it also builds that **know, like and trust** factor with the reader – which… is when they're most likely to email or call you for help!

A **call to action** (CTA) is the single most important part of a blog – for *you*!

You've just spent a few minutes sharing your knowledge for free in a blog to build the **know, like and trust** factor with your audience, but now you want to lead the reader further into how they can tap into this knowledge and expertise even more by working with you. So, if you've written a blog post containing tips on how to schedule Facebook posts, and this is a service you also offer to take away from people's to-do lists, it would be great to end your blog with something like:

> *'I appreciate that scheduling takes a lot of time out of your business, so if this is something you're looking to outsource, take a look at my social media management packages (link to service) created just for small business owners like you.'*

How often should you blog?

I'd recommend blogging at least once a month. I think there's nothing worse than visiting someone's blog and finding they've produced three in quick succession three years ago and then nothing. What would your impression be if you saw that?

Exactly.

Email Marketing

Everyone starts at zero

~

Let me ask you this question: *Which are your two favourite social media channels for business?*

Just prior to writing this chapter, I asked my LinkedIn audience that same question and included an image of the logos of four popular channels to get people thinking and responding.

Most people could answer the question and did indeed give me their favourite two, including their reasons why. However, some who replied only listed one channel, often alongside a comment like, *'I only need one'*.

They were actually the people I wanted to focus on for the purposes of this chapter.

Let me ask you another question:

What if that one platform you use and rely on no longer existed or was no longer available to you?

I think we all now have a greater understanding after COVID-19 that *'what if'* can no longer be ignored, don't we? It's not a negative way to think – it's wholly realistic. You have to think about 'what ifs' because they happen. You can't just coast with blinkers on!

I know it's exhausting, and I know our time is often limited when we're looking after a business, our family, our home, our health, and everything else that comes with life, but we need to plan for the unexpected before something goes wrong.

So, I'll ask again, if you're focusing on just one social media platform, what happens if or when that platform ceases to exist for any reason?

It happens all the time, as well! I don't mean the platform goes bust and Zuckerberg starts selling hotdogs in Disneyland, but that doesn't mean that the platform is still an option for you.

Two scenarios that jump out are these: Your account gets hacked. You can't get into it at best, and someone takes control of it at worst. Or, you don't get hacked, but your account gets taken down. It doesn't actually take a lot to put yourself in a place of not adhering to all the small print, believe me!

Let me tell you what happens if you lose your social media account.

You lose your audience, you lose those people who have bought from you and into you, you lose the relationship you've built with people, you lose potential clients who were so far along that 'know, like and trust' path that they were almost ready to invest in you....

Can you remember them all?

Even if you can, you don't actually have permission to get in touch with them via other non-platform means.

You effectively have to start from scratch.

Ouch.

Of course, if you've already got a full book of clients, you're okay, aren't you? Well okay, but we all know that you can lose them, too – and at any time. Something can happen globally quicker than you can reset your car clock. Or, you could get ill and you won't have the time or the energy to rebuild an audience from scratch.

So today is a good day to start thinking about how you can create another place for your audience to stay in touch with you – and you in touch with them.

Remember that even if you've got multiple platforms, they're never yours. As I said earlier in the book when we looked at the importance of having a website, social media is not a good substitute in the fact that it can disappear at any time.

This is why, despite not actually signing up for many newsletters myself, I am a big fan of email marketing as a way to communicate with and sell to my audience.

Before I continue, remember… *Everyone starts at zero.*

Having a newsletter list is right up there as one of the most valuable resources your business can have.

Why?

Because it's yours! You built it and people came to you because they chose to. Whereas, your audience on social media often contain family, friends, competitors you're keeping an eye on (or vice versa), or people who once liked one of your things. There's a lot of dead wood in your social media following, I'm sorry to say, and most of them will never buy.

This is why you need to build an audience away from social media. Not instead of – as well as!

Here's how…

Sign up to a free email marketing platform like Mailchimp – there are many platforms out there that are free until you reach a certain size of audience and Mailchimp is one of them.

You then need to create a sign-up form for people to add their details to your subscriber list. If you go with Mailchimp, they do have 'help' pages, but they're less than helpful if I'm honest and they're more than a bit jargon-filled, so check out my YouTube channel for tips, or book a Power Hour with me and we can go through everything together.

I teach email marketing as part of my Expert Membership, and as an approved Mailchimp expert / partner, you know you're in safe hands! Yes, that's a thing.

Once you have your sign-up form, that's it, you can now start building that list of subscribers from zero to infinity (note to self; don't type *and beyond*, Catherine. It's not your phrase, and you're already on Disney's watchlist…)

That's it?

Well, okay, no not quite. We've now got to tell people to sign up, but it's okay, you don't need to stand on a roundabout, brandishing a banner made from a cardboard box.

So how?

Tell people

If people aren't signing up to your mailing list, there's usually one thing that's stopping them… You didn't tell them about it.

Have the sign-up link everywhere!

- Email signature

- Social media bios

- Recurring social media posts

- Pop-ups on your website*

- Separate menu tab for 'newsletter' on your website

- Newsletter sign-up in your website footer

- A short and easy to type-in URL on any business cards

- Hell, even get it printed on a t-shirt if that takes your fancy

*Personally, I am not a fan of pop-up boxes, so I was reluctant to add one to my website, but it's actually the biggest converter! So, I guess I'm saying don't dismiss anything until you've given it a good run.

Consider your wording

'Sign up to my newsletter here!'

No, you're alright thanks. Why should I? Tell me why I should. What's in it for me?

We're very reluctant to just hand over our email addresses these days, when in the past it's been the route to receiving spam – and lots of it. So, tell your potential subscribers why they would benefit from signing up.

Maybe you'll regularly share tips to help them overcome their pain points? Or maybe you're offering a 'how to' in exchange for their email address? All free downloads should be given in exchange for an email address so that you can contact them again in future. No longer allow anyone to download anything from you unless they're giving you their email address in return. They're obviously interested in what you've got to offer, so once you've got their email address you can schmooze them (within reason) towards your paid-for services. Captive audience.

Make the sign-up process easy

One big barrier to people joining your list is a lengthy sign-up process. People are busy!

If you're in the UK you do not need double opt-in – where people have to confirm they really did intend to sign up. It's not a legal requirement (at the time of publication), and it's utterly pointless and time consuming.

> *'Thanks for your email address, but are you sure you wanted to give me it, or was it a mistake? Click this second or maybe third button to confirm you're not an idiot...'*

If someone is interested in signing up because you have something they want, then let them have it – ASAP. Don't give them extra unnecessary work to do. You might lose them.

If you're using a piece of software like Mailchimp, you can see where people have signed up from, including their location too, sometimes (it's a stalker's paradise), so you can monitor which channels are converting the best for you.

Make the sign-up form simple

When getting people to sign up, you only need a person's email address really, don't you? I do recommend that you get their first name too though, so you can personalise correspondence, but that's it. Stop there!

You do not need a check box on your sign-up form asking people to confirm they want to receive your emails via email, because that's why they're signing up! Similarly, you don't need to put GDPR questions on there, either. Again, these people are adults, and they don't need you to stoop down in front of them asking, *'Are you sure you know what you're doing?'*

You also don't need their home address. That's just weird and completely off-putting. What are you going to do with it? Send round the heavies if they unsubscribe?

Never do that.

Make the sign-up page less busy

Does the sign-up page also link to lots of other things, like your blog? Get rid of any extra noise and just make the main thing the main thing. I'll come back to that phrase later on.

You just want people to give you their email address at this point. You can distract them once they've signed up with your cleverly placed **Thank You For Signing Up** page!

My YouTube account has some videos on how to do the fiddly bits using Mailchimp – go have a look.

Entice people

We all feel so much better when we have a resolution, an explanation, or a clear path, don't we?

I currently send out business tips to my audience every fortnight, something that – if they implement them – will help to build and grow their business. It costs me only my time to send them but helps show my expertise and keeps me in people's line of sight.

Let's give that to your customers. Think about their pain points and address them in a free download in exchange for their email address. This is called a lead magnet, which we've already touched on.

Some lead magnet ideas you could create could be:

- 'How to' guides

- Cheat sheets

- Checklists

Growth

True story (well, conversation) coming your way...

I've got a mailing list but no one ever signs up.

Oh, when did you last share the sign-up link?

Good question, probably never.

You need to be constantly growing your newsletter list. Even if you have thousands of people already on there, you will still lose people, so you need to be replacing them before they leave.

I share my newsletter sign-up form at least once a week, and it's also on a tab on the menu of one of my websites. It's a pop-up on both of my websites and it's also in my email signature. In addition, it's in my bio on a couple of my social media profiles and regularly goes out on my social media via my scheduling software, so when I say at least once a week – it really is 'at least'.

As I said earlier, most people sign up via my pop-ups, but if I create a particularly triggering lead magnet that resonates with the pain points people feel around my services, I get a whole load of sign-ups from that.

'How To Get Clients' has been my biggest success in this area and I continue to share that lead magnet despite me creating it back in 2018.

I've had a lead magnet bomb, where hardly anyone signed up to it, despite me promoting it just as much as the 'How To Get Clients' download. The unpopular one was a free social media planner, because as a business owner in today's world we need to be active on social media, as you know. But the lack of interest told me that my audience weren't seeing the benefit of having a social media plan, even though this is why many new business owners don't get clients, so I turned that content into a couple of blog posts and added my newsletter sign-up at the bottom of those instead. Voila! Sign-ups were much better than with the social media planner itself.

Like I've said again and again; everyone starts at zero – no subscribers, no followers, no likes. One of the first people to sign up to my mailing list was my Mum (she's been retired 30+ years, so whatever I had to say about business was of no interest to her, really), and one of the first subscribers to regularly reply to my emails was – you've guessed it –

my Mum! To be honest, she probably replies to Costa when they send through her points balance. I'm not special.

But I had to start somewhere. We all do.

The key is to not only keep growing your subscriber list, but also to keep an eye on the engagement. I had a great open rate and really good click rate for the first few weeks, but this was because my retired Mum was clicking everything there was to click! So, she had to go (she was unsubscribed, not actually disposed of from my life). I needed real stats.

What percentage of people are opening your newsletter? Is it the same people every time? Is it your competitors? What percentage are clicking the links in the email and what was the leading text that made them do it? What works for your audience? What size emails have the most unsubscribes? Did your tone of voice change at any point?

Ask yourself those questions and get analysing to see what's working for you – and what isn't.

Testing, Testing, 1.2.3

Test all emails before they get sent. There's nothing worse than links that don't work. People receiving them rarely tell you because they're busy. Plus, it's a bit awkward sending a 'whoops here's the link' follow-up email. Worse still, it attracts unsubscribers as people think you're either sending too much – or just not very professional.

Open

It's all very well getting that perfect newsletter written and sent, but you need to get the recipients to open the blighters. That all starts with the right subject headings.

Remember when you used to return to a full inbox after a holiday and you'd delete the emails you could obviously ignore? Some people made that job so easy for you, by putting 'newsletter' in the subject heading.

Here's your newsletter, Debbie!

Delete! And not just because my name's Catherine.

If someone is time poor, which everyone thinks they are, then you need to grab their attention with something that makes them think, *'Ooooh I need to open that bad boy'.*

So, here are some tips on how to get your newsletter noticed as soon as it lands in someone's inbox.

This is what you want to do to your audience:

- You want to get their attention

- You want to use a bit of clickbait, but...

- You also want them to be in the right mindset and have a jist of the content

- You want to give them something they need

- You want to make people feel special – imagine you're a radio presenter... good DJs make you think you're the one they're talking to, not millions of other people

Let's look at some common scenarios:

Don't worry if the examples aren't within your service area, as this is more about understanding how you make the recipient feel.

You're running an event / webinar / online course

Think about the mindset these two subject headings will put you in:

1. *Invitation to networking event in [your area]*

2. *Are you free next Wednesday?*

Number 1 will likely make you think; *'Oh, sod off'*, or, *'I'll read that later'*, and then you probably won't even think of it again.

Number 2 will raise your blood pressure because you'll think you're being invited somewhere. It looks personal – and you want to know what it is!

You want to thank people for coming to your event / webinar, and possibly sell something else:

Which subject headings will make you want to open the email, and which ones make you think, *'Here we go...'*, or *'go away, we literally just left each other...'*

Example: *Follow up from our meeting / webinar / event*

Yawn! Nobody needs a synopsis of what they were already in attendance for. That's so boring. *'Let's discuss what you already know'*. No, let's not.

Instead, try something that's going to make them think the email contains something new and something that's just for them – remember the DJ analogy I mentioned earlier?

Here's the link I promised you, Catherine.

Thanks for joining me for lunch today.

I use the second one to follow up after I've run a webinar (it helps that I run it at lunchtime) and it always gets a great open rate.

You want someone to do something that only benefits you – perhaps leave a review:

How did we do? (you know before you open it that it's going to be needy)

Second chance to leave feedback (this is a real one I've seen recently – whoopee doo, thanks for making sure I don't miss out, guys!)

When I first started my YouTube channel, I asked my audience to subscribe to it. I had a goal to get to 100 subscribers in a month so that I could have a unique URL. People LOVE to help and they love to be part of a cause – even if that's getting your numbers up for you.

So, I used the following:

I've set myself a goal, can you help? (ooh, yeah)

Do you want to come on a journey with me? (where we going?)

As a result, I got to over 100 subscribers in less than two weeks.

As I said, people LOVE to help. Just let them know why you're asking, what difference it will make, and how grateful you are. You'll find that good people will jump on board.

Something isn't selling well, and you want to raise a bit more interest:

I did this recently for a client. An event wasn't selling and we needed to know why. We needed feedback.

Which email subject would make you want to open it – bearing in mind you probably already knew the event was on?

Tickets still available for the Halloween party.

Last chance to buy your tickets for the Halloween party.

Trying the old *'last chance to buy'* wasn't going to look good if the event was later cancelled through lack of sales.

So, I used…

We're not sure what we've done, but we really need your help.

I then made the content of the email (more about content in a bit) all about how they'd created an event, but *'We must have done something wrong as we've not sold enough tickets to cover the cost of the DJ, party bags, drinks and hall decoration.'* I then asked, *'Is there anyone you know who would like to come along, or is there something we can change?'*

The feedback started coming in. It turned out that the age range for the event didn't work for families with smaller children. So, we changed the age bracket and the event sold out!

You want to sell something new:

Online coaching course now available!

Join my membership today!

presses delete

Neither of these statements directly talk to me, and they've gone straight in with totally trying to sell me something. Yes, people like to buy, but they also need to know why they should invest in your particular thing. Although you can list all of that in the content, that's utterly pointless if people aren't opening the email in the first place.

So, how about we…

a. Think about what your product or service gives to the buyer.

b. Talk about what the end result will be.

For example, my Mailchimp webinars allow people to learn how to navigate around Mailchimp; understanding all the jargon, setting up their own templates and sign-up forms, and sending newsletters with ease. But, I can't put all that in the subject heading. Instead, I think about the problems my webinars solve and test a few different subject headings.

So, I would use something like:

How are you getting on with Mailchimp?

How to understand Mailchimp – easily.

You'll be sending newsletters confidently by the end of this – promise.

Extra bonus tips:

- Don't be afraid to split your audience and test a couple of different subject headings

- Personalise the subject heading, for example: *Catherine, this is for your birthday*

- Avoid spammy words and characters in the subject heading, like: FREE, Bitcoins, $$, ££

Content

So, once you're getting the emails open, what about the content?

You want to sell something sometimes, right? Otherwise what's the point in nurturing your audience?

Consider these points when writing your next newsletter:

- Always make the content enjoyable (something you'd want to read yourself)

- Always give the recipient something (I'm thinking advice rather than discounts)

- Always make it brief (nobody has time to read a lengthy email, and if they do, they're probably not busy and thus won't have cash to spend with you anyway)

- Try and get a conversation going (so ask a question – just one – and invite people to hit reply with their answer)

- Always have a call to action

- Include a brief 'about me' section at the bottom of your email, in case someone signed up on a whim and doesn't really have a clue who you are

Remember, people have provided their email addresses and are trusting you not to spam them. Give them quality newsletters and your open rates will soar.

Strategy

You really need to understand your audience to capture their attention. You need to resonate with them, and you need to show you understand them.

When I did my teacher training back in 2001, one turning point for me was when the lecturer said, *'Step back to when you didn't know what you know now'*. In other words, think about all you have learned on the way to knowing what you know today about the service you provide. Imagine your audience are *now* where you were *then*.

You're going to teach them, impart your knowledge, share your expertise, and show them that you are the person they can trust with their money and business.

You're almost going to teach them that they can do it all themselves – and some will – but lots won't because they don't have time, can't adapt to doing the things that you do, or just can't be bothered with it all. That's great – because they are the ones who'll buy your services after becoming convinced you're the expert.

Consider having some sort of series people can follow – it helps you to manage the relationship and stops you having to talk to all of your audience at once. For example, if you are a social media manager, your series could start with the basics, and then lead them through subsequent tips on how to really grow an engaged paying audience. If your business is copywriting, you could start the series by teaching people how to find their voice, and then throw out valuable content each and every week to help them fully establish it.

Your aim is to build relationships, not to sell to someone as soon as they sign up to your newsletter. You're also not selling clothes, so we're not getting people to sign up with the promise of a '10% discount code'. Nope.

Only send a newsletter when you have something valuable to say. I hate to be the bearer of bad news, but your audience aren't going to be sitting there every other Tuesday waiting for your newsletter to arrive at 10am. If anything, your audience will be waiting to hit unsubscribe if it's another newsletter from you that's as dull as dishwater and ruining their (every other) Tuesday.

Show you're the expert, add value, teach / impart knowledge, but lead people to how they can work with you, too.

Design

Some email accounts don't allow the download of images unless the recipient has that feature turned on or clicks the feature to 'show images', so be mindful of this in your design.

I've recently switched to sending plain text emails with no images. There's been no loss of engagement or open rates, which makes my newsletters now so much quicker to put together. Less work and no altered outcome.

Don't get hung up on your design unless your business is in the creative space, or if you know you're appealing to people who are more visually motivated. It really is about the content because that's what converts

Be consistent in the way your newsletter looks so that people get to remember you, even if it's just having your logo at the top of the email or a tagline at the end that's unique to you and your brand.

Add value, save unsubscribes!

Community

I call my newsletter subscribers my 'newsletter community' and even avoid using the word 'subscribe' on the sign-up button. I instead choose 'submit' or 'sign me up' or 'join the community'. This isn't to trick people. It's to make it look less spammy and more friendly.

Talk to your community as if they're one person.

When my first book was nominated for its second award (like how I slipped that in there?) and I was hopeful for votes from my audience, none of my newsletters started with, *'I've been nominated for...'* or *'Vote for me...'*. They started by taking my community on the journey with me, saying how I had them to thank for even having the book nominated, because without their purchases, Amazon reviews, and support over on social media, the book may not have ever been recognised. I then asked, if they had a moment, whether they could vote for my book in a three-minute survey. I also told them when the winners would be announced.

I won, for the second year running, and thanked my subscribers again for their votes in another newsletter. I showed I cared. They knew it was important to me to win, but I also wanted them to know how important they are to me and how they actually won this award for me, too!

Ouch – dealing with unsubscribers

Now, it's going to hurt when people unsubscribe initially, but isn't it better that you only have people on your list who want to listen to you? Those who are interested in what you have to share and are interested in becoming an investor in your services? This is a good thing.

Don't automatically think that people unsubscribe because you're an awful salesperson or you're doing something wrong. People's direction changes frequently. Maybe they're no longer in business, maybe they don't have the money to invest, maybe they've been ill or dealing with a far bigger issue, maybe they had a baby? We really never know what's going on in people's lives, so don't automatically assume that you've done something wrong.

If you're losing a high percentage of subscribers every time you send an email, though, have a look back through previous newsletters and see if your tone or content has changed dramatically – maybe you've lost your flow? Has your business direction changed? Are you selling different services to what you were when these people first joined your list?

Be thankful that they've left if they're never going to be an engaged member of your community, because nobody likes talking to people who don't listen, do they?

I said, nobody likes talking to people who don't listen… Oh, I give up!

Next chapter…

Pricing and Charging

'I just want to give back'

Okay, but make sure your own oxygen is covered first!

~

As small business owners, we learn early on that we don't have to work with anyone we don't want to. That's one of the many benefits of being your own boss and often a reason why people go into business in the first place.

So why do so many business owners accept less than okay payment terms?

I've worked with a few small business owners to get unpaid invoices sorted out; some months and months old. Often, when I ask why they're only chasing now, months on, the answer is, *'Oh their payment terms are 60, 90, 120 days, it's normal for large companies'.* It might be normal for them – but it's not for you!

Recently, when I was chasing an unpaid invoice of my own, the reply was, *'Our payment terms are 30 days.'*

My response? *'Oh right, well mine aren't!'*

'Their' and 'Our' is the important word here. **Their/Our payment terms.** What makes their terms the right ones? If someone has asked to work with you, they can abide by the terms of your business. If you lapse on one rule, what's to say they won't walk over you on the other ones, too?

It's unacceptable for you as a small business not to be paid on your terms, and it's not your problem if the client can't manage their accounting to pay you in good time.

I know sometimes it feels like, *'Well it's work and so I'd be daft not to take it on their terms'*, but remember – this is your business, your rules. You are not a big corporation, you don't have endless income streams, you don't have departments to do your chasing for you – your terms are your terms, and they keep you in business.

'It's just the way it is, it's normal for big businesses to have longer payment terms'.

Great. It was also normal in the 60s for unmarried mothers to be put into children's homes miles from their families and have their babies removed, but things change. This happened to my Mum. It's not okay just because it happens.

If you're happy to accept poor payment terms because 'they' are a large company, maybe see if the same works next time you're at the supermarket. Bag it all up and then tell the checkout operator you'll be back in four months to pay. You buy from the supermarket – you buy on their terms. The same should go for when people buy from you.

What are your payment terms?

We all need money, but more than anything, we need less stress.

My terms are seven days following completion, or 75% upfront for new clients. This is clear in my terms and conditions. I used to have it set for 14 days, but when I did my AAT2 bookkeeping course a lightbulb came on (an energy efficient one, of course).

If your terms are 14 days and the client doesn't pay on time, you could well be 52 days of work in to the project before you see any money from them!

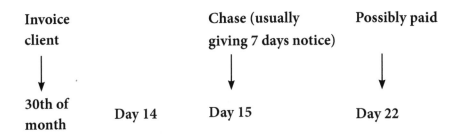

Invoice client		Chase (usually giving 7 days notice)	Possibly paid
30th of month	Day 14	Day 15	Day 22

So you've worked a whole month up to the 30th, then it's another 22 days until you're paid.

If you've continued to work for that client, that's 52 days of paid work you've done for them – and another invoice is due in 8 days!

Now, if your terms are 30 days, you're invoicing for another month's work on the day you're due to be paid for the first one, so if they've not paid the first invoice you're two months without money from the start. Are you okay with that?

I've seen people online saying, *'My invoice is now 6 months overdue'*. WTAF, why did you let it even get that far? Set your payment terms to seven days so you can chase on day 8. Start adding interest as soon as you can, too. Check the UK government website for the latest amount you can add to your invoices. Yes, the government actually tell you to add interest – it's not me being a diva! So, do it!

I've heard people say, *'I let it go, I'm the bigger person'*. You're not the bigger person, you're the poorer one. You've given someone something for free and made them richer in the process through the outcomes.

You could even have your payment terms set to payment on receipt or pay up front. Your business, your rules! There's absolutely nothing stopping you setting your payment terms at 2 hours, if you want. After all, that's how quickly a faster payment transaction goes through the bank.

As it says on the UK government website (correct at time of publication):

> 'You can set your own payment terms, such as discounts for early payment and payment upfront.
>
> Unless you agree a payment date, the customer must pay you within 30 days of getting your invoice or the goods or service.
>
> You can use a statutory demand to formally request payment of what you're owed.'

If you're going to change your payment terms to protect you and your income a little more, how about adding something like this to your terms so it's clear from the start of your relationship:

'My payment terms are seven days. On day 8, interest is charged at 8% plus the Bank of England base rate.'

Again, as the government website also says: *'You have the right to charge interest for late payment'*.

The interest is well warranted, because you should always consider your time spent chasing these charlatans – your time is money, remember. Plus, it's stressful!

'But they'll just go elsewhere if I don't agree to their terms'.

Okay, so be it. You now have room for someone who does respect the needs of a small business owner. You cannot be living off your overdraft, because that is debt and debt accrues interest.

You cannot be living hand to mouth, so don't let anybody force that hand.

This is an important part of creating a safe, sustainable and profitable business – the whole tagline of this book!

Ways to avoid late payers

It's never going to be 100% unavoidable, as we all know problems can occur for anyone at any time. But, there are a few things you can put into practice to limit the chances of late payment and subsequent issues with your stress and cashflow:

- Ask for money upfront – whether it's a percentage of the final bill or 100%. A lot of business owners decide on this option after being stung more than once.

- Be sure to set and agree your payment terms and the full cost in writing (this includes email), before you start any job, so the client has the opportunity to allocate that money in their account.

- Don't hand over completed work to new clients – wait until full payment is received or the work is approved in writing.

Increasing your prices

It's so hard increasing your rate, isn't it? And this is one reason why we don't give discounts (but more on that later). It's also another reason why always knowing your outgoings, as discussed in the Know Your Hourly Rate chapter, is important. Outgoings can and will change regularly. That monthly utilities bill you pay by direct debit just went up. That cooker that you thought had another few years left in it just went pop. Your prices? They need to go up!

Plus, the economy dictates our prices sometimes, too. Inflation.

But, it's hard to up your prices, isn't it?

What if you lose clients? Or what if nobody wants to pay your new rate, ever?

Just leave it, yeah? It's not worth the hassle or the anxiety, right?

Well, yeah you can think like that, but please then remember that as well as wanting to make a nice profit, you also need to be covered in the absence of sick pay, holiday pay, pension contributions, taxes, outgoings… You have to cover all of these things yourself.

Therefore, you deserve to earn what you're worth plus a little bit more, because you're good at what you do!

Here's how to up your prices and feel confident about it:

1. Update your website

The first thing to do is update your website and online material with your new prices. Do NOT add *'discounted until XXX'*. That's you thinking you're not worth it – subliminally.

I suggest starting with your website as you can then see that the world doesn't implode by adding some different numbers to your pricing.

2. Contacting previous clients

You're not only going to tell existing clients that your hourly rate is increasing, but anyone who has ever used your services in the past, so dig out those previous client email addresses now.

Previous clients need no notice period, they get the new rate straight away – lucky devils!

Here's an example of what I have sent to previous clients in the past:

> *Tom* (always personalise it)
>
> *It was an absolute pleasure working with you last year!*
>
> *And, it would be an equal pleasure working with you again in 20**, but before we do, I wanted to let you know that I have recently*

increased my hourly rate / price for the service you used (name service so it's personal) to £XX an hour.

I hope that if and when the need arises for you to have support from me again, this new price works with your budget.

Speak soon.

Catherine

Note, there is no apology here, and I'm not wasting their time with fluff or the insincere, *'How are you'*. It's to the point, relevant and not a big intrusion into their busy day.

This isn't only a great way to let them know your rate has increased, but also a great opportunity to remind them you exist and get back on their radar.

Make sure you include a line about any new services you've introduced that they may like to use since you last worked with them.

3. Contacting existing clients

Okay, this is the scary one. I know, I appreciate that, so maybe don't tell them all the good news in one hit. Let's do it one by one to see what the comeback is.

It might feel easier to do this when you've started taking on new clients at the new prices, but do ensure you can actually take on new clients and that all your time isn't taken up with lower paying clients at this point. If that's the case, start with the one you don't mind getting rid of – just in case they do have a problem with you charging a bit more. You know, that client who always has an 'urgent' job but then disappears when you drop everything to do it, or that client who starts every email with, 'I'm not being funny, but...'. The client who makes your stress levels increase whenever you see their name flashing on your phone... we've all had them!

Get-out clause... you may want to keep existing clients on their old hourly rate but consider if that means you can't take on any additional clients on the new rate. If so, you do need to up their prices otherwise you're stuck forever. Or perhaps the client on your old rate takes up more than 20% of your time? Then they definitely need to go on your new rate or be outsourced to another contractor – more on that in the Outsourcing and Automation chapter.

Here's how I worded one of my last emails. Stick to the truth – don't try to call anyone's bluff:

> *Hi {personalised}*
>
> *I put my hourly rate up from £35 to £40 in January 20** – but that was for new customers only, the lucky devils!*
>
> *Since then, my business has been going from strength to strength, to the point where I am turning people away.*
>
> *So, I now have to bring everyone onto the same hourly rate.*
>
> *It's an absolute joy working with you and I thoroughly love every element of it, so I hope that we can continue to work together throughout 20**.*
>
> *The increase will take effect from 1st February 20**.*
>
> *If you have any questions, please let me know.*
>
> *Catherine Gladwyn*

Note again: no apology, no negotiation, no explanation for the increase... your business, your rules.

Now! Enjoy the extra money!

Retainers

I'm aware that many business owners like to have their clients on retainers, but they really aren't the be all and end all. They can often be a cloud over a business owner's sense of building a relationship and the service they provide, as it just becomes about the money and the time.

I know, I know, if clients are on retainers you know what's coming in every month... BUT, this is only the case providing everyone pays their invoice, doesn't go out of business themselves, or doesn't suddenly decide to stop working with you! Anything can happen, and having someone on a retainer makes zero difference unless all other factors are ticking along nicely.

Let's refer back to COVID-19 and Carillion. Many small businesses have got lots of unpaid bills due to Carillion collapsing. They won't be anywhere near the top of the creditors list, sadly. That retainer means nothing.

Many clients want to work with you in small bits to begin with because they want to get to know you. Many are handing over elements of their business – the business they've taken possibly years to grow – to a complete stranger. It's unrealistic to expect someone to find your website and want to invest in 20 hours a month without even knowing how you work.

I worked with a subcontractor who kept on and on at me to go on a retainer and, totally unlike me, I gave in – against my better judgement! I couldn't guarantee I'd have enough work for them every month, so I immediately felt uncomfortable about it and panicked about finding her work. I'm not sure if it was me, or them, but I found their standard of work went right down as soon as the retainer was paid, and I am not entirely convinced they used the hours as well as they did when we were just working on an ad hoc basis. There was nothing in this new arrangement 'for me', so I stopped working with them.

But, the positive was that it gave me an insight into how clients feel if we're badgering them to go onto a retainer.

Carole Searle is a member of my Expert Membership. She felt she turned a corner in her business when she stopped focusing on getting clients on retainers. Here's her story (so that you can have a nice little break from me, for a while):

What were your thoughts on retainers before you started being mentored by me?

I'd always been made to feel that retainers were the epitome of success; like I'd made it as a business owner if I'd got a client on a retainer.

What are your thoughts now?

My thoughts have now totally changed. You've taught me that it doesn't matter if the client is ad hoc or retainer. What's important is that they are on the right contract for the both of you, relationships are being built, and that you are both happy with how things are progressing.

What made you think differently?

I think I started feeling differently about this once I actually had a couple of retainer clients and realised that there wasn't really all that much difference to ad hoc work. Yes, a retainer is a guaranteed monthly income, but if the client suddenly can't afford to be tied into the commitment for whatever reason, or just can't always find enough work to fill the hours, they're soon going to end the contract and leave you with nothing. So in some ways, it can be easier to just have lots of ad hoc clients which still equate to enough of an income for you.

Do you now see the importance of building a relationship over anything else?

I can see it's really important to build relationships with clients and get to know them and their business properly, so you can then advise on the type of work needed and the amount of time tasks are likely to take, etc. They can then make a more informed decision as to whether a retainer or ad hoc contract is the right choice for them. It can also make these kinds of conversations more comfortable to have with each other, as it makes the client feel more relaxed and not under pressure to commit to more hours if they don't really need or want them. They trust you, which, as you always say, contributes to there likely being a longer-term working relationship anyway.

If I were the business owner who had someone constantly trying to push me into spending money every month that I'm not sure I'll be able to always afford – and for work that I can't guarantee I'll always need doing – it would probably make me feel stressed and resentful of the contract and so I'd eventually want to end it anyway.

Yes, ad hoc work isn't a guaranteed income, but it can be so much better in other ways. It's still an income, and it gives flexibility to your client, which will in return help build a great relationship with them and maybe in the future lead to more work from them when they are in that position. You can take on more work with several different clients, along with a range of different tasks, so that you're not doing the same thing every month or becoming reliant too heavily on one client.

What was the biggest lightbulb moment for you in your mentoring?

The turning point for me was just recently. I had a client who signed up for a retainer (through their own choice) but a few months down the line, they realised that they couldn't afford it due to still being in the early stages of growing their own business. I'd have panicked before because of the 'I must get everyone on a retainer' mindset.

I knew that the client still needed help, though, so I suggested instead of stopping working together totally, why not swap to an ad hoc contract instead and that way, they could just call on my services as and when they needed me – with no commitment on their part to have to guarantee giving me work. They immediately agreed to this as it was a much better solution for them at that moment in time.

They're happy now that there's no pressure on them to provide work all the time, and love that if they do come up with anything that needs doing, they know they can contact me and I will schedule it in for them asap.

Building relationships is far more important than getting clients on retainers, and this is what I help my mentees with. Once you get out of the mindset that retainers are the key to success you will relax a little, and do the one thing that's more important – **building long term relationships, building trust, and creating a model of longevity in your business.**

There are ways to move ad hoc clients onto retainers successfully if you so want to, of course. I do it regularly in my own business and help others to do it as well. If you'd like to work towards that, you can either join my membership or book a Power Hour to work with me one to one.

Should we offer discounts for retainers?

I get asked this a lot, and my question in response is... *'What is your aim?'*

The reply is almost always; *'To get first / more clients'.*

Great, very proactive, but what about your existing clients (if you have them)? What do they think of new customers getting discounts after they've been so loyal to you? Why can't they enjoy a special offer, too?

No – that doesn't mean go and give everyone some money off out of fairness, because that way you'll be working day and night to recoup the lost income.

If you start doing new deals for new clients, then people will see your sector as disposable and just shop around for a deal rather than the service. I've phoned Sky TV and threatened to leave knowing I'll get some money off, and I know most of my friends have done similar, too. We don't want our clients to start doing that to us, though. Sky are massive – we are not.

What would you think if you were looking for an accountant and one had a 'special offer'? I know not everyone will agree with me here, but I'd think it's unprofessional.

You're selling your time and expertise, not a product you knocked up for a couple of quid.

Remember that in charging less, you're going to have to work more to recoup it. And, of course, you don't want one client taking up more than 20% of your time, or your income, do you?

But to answer the question properly; let's say your hourly rate is £30, and you're sending a potential client an email to offer your services, and you go in with:

'My hourly rate is £30, but if you take five hours a month, I'll knock off 20%'

Here's why that's a mistake:

1. You're already showing the potential client that there's room to haggle and that you don't even think you're worth £30 an hour.

2. As we discussed a moment ago, who wants five hours a month straight off without getting to know you? Not many clients, that's for sure.

3. How are you going to get back a whole lost hour in income?

4. Will the client want to stay with you when you realise all of the above and want to change the terms, or were they just interested pure and simple in the discount?

5. What if an existing client wants more hours? They'll want that same discounted hourly rate that goes down with every extra chunk of five hours, won't they?

6. It doesn't lead to longevity – you'll end up with clients who can't actually afford your hourly rate and are just taking you up on the discount.

Your rate is non-negotiable, regardless of who or what the client or occasion is. If you reduce your rate, you earn less for the same time. That's the outcome.

If you believe in you, others will too

You need to believe in your rates. If you are seen to be reducing it here, there and everywhere, it looks a little desperate and people will begin to avoid or question your full rate.

Set your rate and stick to it until you need to increase it. If you're not getting clients, it's highly unlikely that it's your hourly rate that's stopping people. It's usually a catalogue of things, with the main one being that you don't believe in your prices.

Don't forget…

Running a sustainable, profitable business does not happen overnight. You **will** get more paying clients, you can make this a viable business with a regular income and profit, but it will not happen overnight (or even in a week!)

Ignore everyone online who declares they're making six figures and were smashing it before they even woke up. I'm not saying they're not, but even if they are (and chances are slim), their life and desires are not going to be the same as yours, so ignore, admire, block or whatever you want to do, then focus on your own goals.

Discounts

It's inspiring to see business owners thinking of ways to attract their first or new paying clients, but some can become so focused on getting them that they'll start making decisions that can affect the longevity of their business – like offering discounts!

Here's why I believe, from observing and assisting other business owners and those I mentor, that discounts are not going to help your growth. In fact, I think it could set you back considerably.

'I've only been in business a little while'

Nobody is paying you for the length of time you've been registered with HMRC – they're paying you for the service you provide and the change you make for them.

You don't charge people less because you're learning how to manage a business – that's got absolutely nothing to do with the services you offer.

Let me put it this way...

'Oh yeah, I will be charging £30 an hour but not until I know exactly where I want my expense receipts to be kept – on the bookcase, in my purse or on a notice board'.

You will learn how to be a business owner in your own time, but none of that will reflect on the services you provide your clients with.

'I'm not very confident with the service I've been asked to provide'.

Whoa! Back up, back up. Say, what? Why are you saying yes to something you can't do with confidence? Would you engage someone to fix your boiler if they said they weren't sure what to do, but will charge you less as a result? This is both of your reputations on the line, here.

'I'm charging below my competitors to get the work'.

It's a bit cruel, enticing clients knowing you're going to up your rates at some point. Also, your competitors will notice what you're doing and you won't be very popular. You need to keep them onside. You can contribute to bringing the market rate down if you charge less, as that's how the economy works. I know people do it, but that doesn't make it right.

Business owners don't do discounts. Furniture stores do discounts!

Discounts very, very rarely convert into full paying clients, if at all.

Just sell what you're selling – at the right price.

There are hundreds of people providing the same services as you and getting work at their full price. It's not your full hourly rate that's stopping you getting clients.

Free stuff

'I want to give my time for free because I like to give back'.

To who? Who are you helping? The time you spend working for free is better spent doing things to find paying clients.

During COVID-19, one woman's dog-walking business went under because a load of people in the community were offering to walk people's dogs for free so they could get out and because they wanted to 'give back'. These dogs were already being walked, but this woman was charging for it as it was her business and she was insured! Now that a freebie was on the table elsewhere, sadly, she suffered financially on a large scale.

My point is this. If you are trying to 'give back', please consider those who you're taking away from.

Packages

What is a package?

In a nutshell, it's a group of tasks or services you can provide for existing or potential clients.

Why do I need packages?

How often does an enquiry land in your inbox / social media messenger account that says, *'Tell me what it is you do?'*, *'How much will this cost?'* or *'What does that service involve?'*

Or perhaps you get enquiries and don't know how to price them? Maybe you're undercharging or overcharging and nobody is working with you as a result?

The customer journey has to be as easy as possible. Imagine going online to buy your weekly shop and find that there's a package where it's all done for you. You just pay £250 and you'll have 'everything you need for a whole week'! But that's it, no other information. Is it even the stuff you asked for? Is it delivered the next day? Does it include alcohol?

Now imagine going online for your weekly shop and it lists what will be in the shopping, what time it'll be delivered, and announces that there will even be bonus recipe cards with it. Hell, you can even have a chef! That's more like it, you know what you're getting and what the outcome will be for your investment.

As a business owner yourself, you need to remember that it's hard giving over your hard-earned cash at any time. You need to know what you're getting in return. It can't be vague, which is why packaged services are so good for your clients and a way to stop short-changing yourself because you 'panic price' things.

Since introducing packages for some of the services in my own business, I found an increase in enquiries for those specific services and received comments on numerous occasions like, *'I've come to you as I know what I am getting for my investment'.*

I had created a new and exciting service for my business and wanted to attract new customers, obviously. But I felt I needed to ask potential clients questions before I could give them a price, which meant they would need to contact me.

Catherine suggested this was a little too much effort for people and also a bit awkward as people might think I'm out of their price range or not realise how much my services are worth.

I toyed with the idea of having a 'starting from' pricing point, but Catherine said no – again!

Instead, she suggested I have three offerings; three different prices, all with clear details on what the services provide.

This makes it so much easier for people and makes it easier for me to talk about my pricing, too.

– Amy Nolan

What do packages need to include?

- They need to be clear – what is the client getting?

- They need to be priced properly – don't short-change yourself or price yourself out.

- They need to be relevant – think about what your audience likely needs from this service.

- Avoid jargon – for example, if you're offering bookkeeping or website support packages. Avoid the terms some business owners don't understand or want to understand.

For more information on how to create packages for your service-based business, you'll love my course, which is aptly named... How to Create Packages! Head over to catherinegladwyn.co.uk

Myths

Here are some common myths people put in their own way which hinder their progression in business.

'There are others charging less so I need to drop my rates when asked or clients will go elsewhere'

Will they? Will they really? Or is that your perception without ever actually having stuck to your rates every time you think you need to offer a discount?

When you factor in essential and mandatory expenses like insurance, software fees, admin, tax, national insurance, ICO registration, etc., etc., those who charge less are often earning much less than they would be as an employee. It also always makes me question whether they are indeed insured and / or paying taxes, when I see such low hourly rates from UK-based businesses.

Now, this next comment always gets me grief on social media, but I firmly believe that if you start lowering your rate, you'll start bringing everyone down. You'll also attract clients who don't see your worth, and oh boy – are you worth every penny.

As I've already said, your price is also nothing to do with how long you've been in business! Your clients and potential clients aren't paying you on the longevity of your business, they're paying you for the service you provide, your expertise, and the change you make to their life / business.

So, stop looking at others. Ignore that one who thinks she's Mother Teresa and undercutting everyone. No discounts, no special offers.

If you're not getting clients it's not just your price that's a problem, if at all. What else are you not doing? Are you marketing consistently? Are you telling people regularly what it is you do? Does your marketing attract the right people? There's so much more that will be stopping you getting clients. It is not because you need to offer a discount, believe me!

If you're still stuck at the end of this book after implementing everything for longer than an hour, then let's talk via one of my Power Hours.

'I saw your LinkedIn post about knowing your worth and not offering discounts. With regards to the client I won last week, they asked if I charge for the first on-boarding call, bearing in mind they'd already had their free 20 minute call.

I said I did, and he said the three other business owners he had spoken to offered it for free.

He still went ahead with me knowing he'd have to pay, though. So, I know you're telling the truth that you don't have to discount, although I did nearly come close. I could hear you in the background saying, NO!'

– Kellie Simpson

If you want guidance and support to run a profitable long-term business that makes you proud and happy, then thinking you owe others something and putting yourself second is not the way to do it.

I know this is all hard and a bit scary, but the sooner you adopt these methods, the sooner your business becomes safer, more sustainable and profitable. It will give you the joys you hoped for when you first decided to run your own business.

Outsourcing and Automation

*Why pay someone else to do it when you can
do it yourself?*

~

Why outsourcing is important

Richard Reed, co-founder of Innocent Smoothies, spoke at a conference I attended back in 2015, and one thing he said stood out for me; *'Make the main thing the main thing'.*

The main thing for you is the service you provide.

But how can you concentrate on the main thing when you've got all the other tasks to do that come with running a business?

By outsourcing them!

Hang on... didn't you say in the Money Mindset chapter to decrease your outgoings? You're contradicting yourself... now, where's my Amazon app so I can leave you a 1 star review?

Wait! Blimey, you're a live wire!

As a business owner, outsourcing is something that must happen for the growth of your business – and for the reduction of your stress levels. If you bring in someone to do the things you either can't, won't or shouldn't be doing, then you're free to get more clients and do client work that you can charge for! It's not always about work-life balance.

I work with some clients who don't want that work-life balance and thrive on a full to-do list. They like working and they enjoy having the freedom to work even whilst away on holiday, but as your business grows, there will come a time when you have to let some things go because there just aren't enough hours in the day.

By learning to delegate and outsource, you're free to focus your energy on the growth of your business and its needs.

Before we look at what to consider delegating, there are a couple of things I think are important to hold on to, even if you don't enjoy them:

- **Expenditure** – especially if you're a very small business or start-up, you need to keep on top of everything that goes out and comes in to your business, so that you can monitor your cashflow and make changes before there are problems. For example, for the clients I do bookkeeping for, I am in their accounts so often that I can see anomalies pop up, or subscription renewals due, and I can raise these queries to ensure my clients are aware of them. But, if their accounts were being done once a year, it's often too late or too much hassle to do anything about any issues.

- **Future Plans** – make sure you remain the final decision maker on any plans for your business's future. Some decisions can't be undone.

- **Goals** – you need to be setting – and be comfortable with – your own goals. Don't let someone else dictate your end goal. This is your business, so it needs to work for you.

- **Bad press / complaints** – one mishandled and disgruntled client can lead to all manner of problems. Ensure you stay on top of complaints and grievances and deal with them personally. Even the most annoying complainer might have some valid points.

Why should you outsource?

You've been doing it all just fine on your own, and anyway, you can't afford to get someone to do it for you. That sound familiar?

There are many occasions where you will need to outsource in order to make room for new money to come in or to expand your reach. Outsourcing usually frees you up to do even more in your business, or it can provide a return on investment. Sometimes, it does both!

For example, if you bring in an expert to do some Google Ads for you, it's likely not going to be cheap, but… the return on investment should cover it – and more.

Could you achieve the same results yourself?

Probably.

But how long will it take you to learn how to do Google Ads properly? How many mistakes will you make (and have to spend time fixing), how much money will you waste, and if we go back to that 'your time is money' thing I keep banging on about – how much are those Google Ads really costing you?

It's likely it's costing you much more time and money than it would to bring in an expert at the beginning.

Plus, all that time you're spending on learning and swearing at Google Ads is time you can't work with paying clients or be doing other things on / in your business.

'By the time I've told someone what to do, I could have done it myself'

Yes, yes, you're right. It can sometimes take a while to tell someone how to do what you do and have them understand it. But the second time they do it, they won't need telling, and it frees you up to do what brings in the money.

Weigh it up again. How much is it costing YOU to do it, versus how much it costs an expert to do it?

'It's just easier to do it yourself, it's only a few quid saved, right?'

Wrong! That mindset is what's driving down your income and profit. A few quid saved here and there will soon add up.

Let's put it another way. A coffee every day is only a few quid. For that weekly meeting in town, the parking is only a few quid. That lunch en-route to another meeting, that was only a few quid, too. Those few quids all add up to a big quid over time.

And here's another way to look at it. If you're spending so much time in your business on things because you'd 'save a few quid', how much money are you losing because you don't have time to be bringing in new money?

What should you outsource?

This one's easy... It's basically anything you can't, won't or shouldn't be doing.

Can't?

Perhaps it's the bookkeeping. You try to keep on top of it, but you're just creating more work for your accountant and wasting your own time.

You might think you're great at everything, but you're probably best at the services your business provides. Remember, make the main thing the main thing.

You already know there are people who specialise in all sorts of different areas – sometimes, you've got to stick to what you're good at and let others do what they do best.

Won't?

Again, it's likely something like your bookkeeping – or maybe your social media? You start with good intentions and you're pleased with your efforts, but then four weeks into this newfound skill, it's all gone belly up. Come week five, you choose to do anything but the one thing you've now come to loathe.

The first thing I ever outsourced was my cleaning. Absolutely nothing to do with my business, but it had a positive knock-on effect. Someone now comes in every two weeks to clean my house from top to bottom and I am not embarrassed to admit that only the bathroom gets touched in between her visits.

Before I had my cleaner, I was constantly wiping down surfaces, running the vacuum round the living room etc., during my working hours, thinking I was 'keeping on top of it'. I'd also use it as a procrastination tool. But now, I couldn't care less about the crumbs on the carpet or the sock fluff leading up the stairs, because it's not my job! It's the cleaner's job and I pay her for it, so I don't want it already half done when she gets here otherwise I am paying her to do less.

Shouldn't

Can I use bookkeeping again as an example? Great!

I do a few clients' bookkeeping every week, and when I went on holiday once I came back to a friendly email from one client saying, *'I helped. I did the reconciliation while you were away'*.

Even writing it makes my eyes roll with despair. He'd matched things with invoices that were years old… it was chaos in just a week. That's something he *shouldn't* be doing as it took me almost twice as long to undo his 'help', which consequently cost him twice as much. Oh, how we laughed!

You're so much better off spending your time where you can directly bring the money in.

Who to choose

Your branding needs re-doing and you've found a relative of a friend who did GCSE Art 11 years ago. He'll knock something up for fifty quid. Result?

No – or at least, not a good one!

Saving money isn't the way to effectively outsource. You need to find the right people for the right jobs; people with expertise in their area and who know how to work with small business owners. You need to be working with people who are in business themselves, not someone who's looking to make a bit of money on the side because they're a bit bored in their day job and fancy some extra cash for their lads' holiday in Magaluf.

Remember, pay peanuts...

I always say to my mentees, find who you're going to outsource to before it all gets out of hand and overwhelming, otherwise you might make hasty decisions in your selection and you'll have precious little onboarding time. I also recommend you have an admin bible ready to hand over with your processes, as well as a secure password sharing system. I use LastPass.

Remember, you're outsourcing for a reason. If you were bad at it yourself, don't go telling the expert how to do it.

> *Due diligence – ask to speak to previous clients and check their testimonials. If you want to give a new business owner an opportunity, just check what they've done in the past. If they're offering graphic design but have only ever sold fruit and veg and/or*

been on a manual handling course as part of their career, then they may not be the best person for the job you're giving them.

Have a chat with possible people via Zoom. It's not an interview, but you still need to get to know them. Have a look at their online profiles whilst you're there – do you get a good feel for them?

If you're asking other people for recommendations, check whether they've actually worked with them. Some people refer others because they gain from it, or because it's just someone they've seen online and they quite like them, or because they're a friend. Recommendations should only be made if you've had direct experience of their work, in my opinion.

After publishing my first book, my business really took off and I was getting close to the point in my business where I was going to have to be really selective with clients and turn people away unless I could invent more hours. So, the next thing to do was to practice what I preach and outsource, but it was scary!

Finding an associate to work with in my Virtual Assistant business was daunting. I had all the fears that you will have. The main one being that my hard-built reputation would be battered if that person messed up. But, I wasn't giving them my clients – I was keeping the main thing myself, so really I had no excuse but to go for it.

My next concern was how to find 'The One'. We've all seen posts on social media where people ask for a certain professional, and then out come a wave of vultures saying, *'Pick me!', 'I've DM'd you', 'I recommend Dave...',* etc.

So, how do you find 'The One'?

How do you know who to trust?

Who do you narrow it down to?

What do you ask them?

How much do you pay them?

I put a lot of thought into how I could find the right person, as there are sadly some people who like to 'fake it until they make it'. Here's the process I went through to find my help.

Step One

Write down exactly how you're feeling at this time and answer your concerns as if you were speaking to a potential client who might be looking to work with you. You can now imagine how your clients feel when they first consider investing in you, so write a blog post titled something like, 'I know how it feels before you start working with a XYZ' as it shows great empathy and eases people's fears, somewhat.

Step Two

Task

- A4 paper – landscape

- Three columns headed: can't, won't, shouldn't

- Pop all the tasks you do in your business under one of these columns (excluding the main thing that you're good at – the service you provide)

- Now, you have your list of things you need to outsource

You obviously don't have to outsource all of them. I recommend starting with one that comes under the 'can't' column, as this will likely be one that takes up too much of your time and is probably one that stays on your to-do list the longest. Something that requires a skill or a qualification, perhaps.

Step Three

Consider where you're going to look for your expert. I found both of my associates by writing a LinkedIn post. I find the caliber of people able to follow instructions to be far higher over there.

Even though social media can leave you inundated with 'PM me' and 'Pick me' comments, my next tip will help you weed out those who aren't your ideal match.

Step Four

Top secret... put a note on the bottom of your post to say:

> *'No PMs or comments please – only email me if you're interested or can recommend someone.'*

This frees you of having to weed through the pointless comments, and you can instead ignore those who can't follow instructions. Better still, you can choose whether to include your email address in the post or not, so you can test how proactive people are at finding your details and see whether they can work on their own initiative or need constant guidance.

Step Five

I am, for obvious reasons, drawn to any posts that have 'VA' in them, and I see lots that simply say, *'I need a VA'*. What follows is a pitch from everyone who is, wants to be, or thinks they are a VA, replying in droves. But VAs offer a variety of services, so how do you know who to pick if you've not defined what needs doing? And how do those replying know they're the right one for the job without asking for more information?

It's all going to fail from the off, if you ask me.

List in your post the type of skills you're hoping your subcontractor has, along with the kinds of tasks you'd be looking to hand over to them. And, as above, invite them to email you directly – to see how serious they are about the role and how well they can follow instructions. So, if someone comments or PMs you, you can dismiss them straight away as they've not read the post and thus probably won't be too hot on heeding any other instructions you give them, either.

Remember, the person you're looking for will be self-employed – just like you. This isn't a job interview and you don't need a CV. You're going to be working <u>with</u> someone. Don't be bolshy or arrogant or try and tell someone it should 'only take five minutes'.

Step Six

Ask people to only get in touch if they're able to meet all of the requirements in the post, unless you're prepared to pay them to learn on your time, that is. There are some wannabe business owners out there who really should be suffering with imposter syndrome, but sadly, suffer from completely the opposite.

Step Seven

Provide those who get this far (hopefully there are at least some) with a document which fully lists everything you would need help with now and possibly in the future, and how you would like to work with them. One thing I include is that I would hope that the person would reply to my emails within two hours between the hours of 9-5, Monday to Friday. This was just my personal preference when I subcontracted. I didn't want someone who would get back to me two days later with a 'So sorry, my child was ill', because that's not how I work. If that person doesn't want to work on my terms, that's completely fine, but it's a way of you filtering if they're the one for you.

Step Eight

Enjoy going through the replies and make sure you respond to everyone who follows the process, even if you're not selecting them. You'll no doubt remember how it felt when you'd taken the trouble to get in touch with someone and you heard nothing back… don't be that person.

Step Nine

Make sure you get a contract together – I'm afraid I can't advise you any further on that as I am not in any way legally trained. You need one, though, to protect you, your clients and your business.

Getting started

Set clear tasks

It's important to understand what you want before asking someone to do it for you. So, if you would like someone to schedule your social media posts for you, you may need to outline exactly what they'll be responsible for. The initial time spent clearly clarifying what needs doing will save a lot of time and money not having to go back and forth later on:

- All social media accounts?
- Engagement with comments?
- Sourcing images?
- Content research?
- Keywords?
- Calls to action?
- Deadlines?
- Frequency of updates on task?

You're not teaching the expert to suck eggs here, you're simply defining what you're looking for help with. This enables them to do it right. If you leave out any aspects of what you want done, you only have yourself to blame if they don't do something or do it wrong.

When I help clients with diary management, I always ask what days and times they like to hold meetings / have phone calls. It's imperative that I know this, so I don't book a meeting when they usually drop a child off at nursery, for example.

Consider everything, because it'll help you in the long term.

Make sure you listen to the thoughts of your expert, too. They may come up with things you hadn't thought of. They're the expert, and that's why you hired them.

How to delegate

Learning how to delegate better can improve your business and its success.

No need to micro-manage

I know, it's hard not to micro-manage. I worked as a manager at the National Trust and it took me a long time not to over-analyse every task I delegated.

Giving up control is one of the hardest things to do in life (I have no scientific proof of that – it just sounds good). I'm not saying you can't oversee tasks, as it is of course essential you know the job's getting done, but with clear task objectives you should have everything in place for it to go well without you.

A freelancer's time is money, so don't be surprised if the time taken to read and reply to all of those *'How you getting on?'* messages are going on the clock (another reason to avoid micro-managing).

One of the beauties of working with freelancers, as opposed to having employees, is that you don't have to find them work. If you're having a bad month, you can take your work back in-house again.

I never tie-in any of my clients who hire me for their VA work. Nobody needs that stress.

Automation

Now, this excites me! It's so much fun having something in the background doing the things you used to do.

There's a lot of software out there to make your life easier in business, and much of it is available for free on basic packages, which is perfect when you're first getting to know what software you need.

Here are some pieces of software I have to help me run my business, that reduce the amount of time I need to spend doing things that don't really need my input.

Accounting software

My first investment was accounting software, FreeAgent. It was a nice addition having previously created all of my invoices in Word and converted them to PDF. I kept a log of all outgoings and income in a spreadsheet, had to set diary reminders to chase things if they weren't paid, and worried irrationally that I would lose receipts and invoices in a house fire and be in trouble with a very unforgiving HMRC.

That's why I often say that the investment in accounting software was life-changing (and this is coming from someone who, medically speaking, has had their life changed)!

I saved around 4-6 hours a month by investing in that accounting software, which cost £205 for the year. My hourly rate then was £20, so I recouped that investment in less than two months because I could spend the 4-6 hours on client work / getting new clients. I now get the software free for life as I shared an affiliate link at every opportunity!

Calendly

'Are you free at 11 next Wednesday?'

No reply for days.

'Yes, I am!'

At this point, you're no longer free.

'I'm not now. How about Thursday at 2pm?'

48 hours tick past…

'Yes – let's go for that!'

Ugh, Nope – that slot has gone now, too… and you can't see an end to this cycle.

We've all been there. Someone wants to speak to you 'urgently', and so you bend over backwards to accommodate them, only for them to take forever to confirm a date, not turn up for the call, or cancel with three minutes to spare.

So, I get everyone to book a call with me via software that integrates with my calendar – whether it's one of my paid-for calls or a free 20-minute consultation. It all gets done via Calendly. I've implemented this for so many clients, too. All I then have to do is turn up for the call.

I've seen a huge increase in the quality of people booking the calls, a huge decrease in having my time wasted, and very rarely now does someone not turn up or cancel with little notice. I charge for anything above 20 minutes and the software sends them reminders. I also state that 48 hours' notice is needed for all and any cancellations.

The link is on my website, in some social media posts and shared in PMs when someone says, *'Can I just pick your brains...?'*

Zoom

I tried another well-known video conferencing software, but the damned thing kept logging me out and wouldn't let me back in. It was always so stressful having a conference call, so when I found Zoom it made life so much easier.

I didn't need to invest in it straight away as the free plan was enough to hold the odd call (it's currently free for unlimited time between two of you to just have a chat). But as soon as I introduced Power Hours into my business and started hosting webinars or recording me speaking for virtual events, I needed to invest.

I now link my Zoom account with Calendly and Stripe so that anyone who books a call with me gets an automatic link as soon as they've paid – and I don't have to do anything other than show up. Zoom is also integrated with my calendar so I can book meetings myself and a link to join is automatically generated.

It saves so much time and the investment is recouped easily because I charge for my time on Power Hours, webinars, and to speak at/on events.

Stripe

There's another well-known payment collection piece of software which I do not endorse. I used it for years with an online auction site, because I don't think there was a choice back then. I found it very buyer biased. When you're selling digital downloads, courses, ebooks and other things that people can access immediately, you do not want them being able to grab a refund without some consultation with you. In fact, my understanding is that in the UK, digital downloads don't come with the same consumer rights for refunds – but check that in case I am wrong

/ out of date. Stripe is highly reliable and works easily with WordPress plugins – especially WooCommerce – and Calendly. They take less commission from you and the software is so much easier to navigate.

Google Forms

Do you have questions you regularly ask new clients? If so, read on!

I always ask those I provide diary management for some key questions, like…

- Who can't be ignored?

- Who definitely should be ignored?

- What are your family members' names?

- Who's the mistress (joke)

- What is your favourite airline?

- Do you fly economy?

- What are your dietary requirements?

- What are your preferred working hours?

- What time would you be happy to have the first face to face meeting of the day?

- What train station do you live near?

I need these answers in order for me to provide good inbox and diary management, and I need to have them accessible to me frequently until it becomes second nature. So, I ask all of these questions in a Google form, which either gets sent to the client to complete themselves, or we can complete it together on a call.

Social media scheduling software

I've tried a few social media scheduling programmes on behalf of clients over the years and have recently invested in MeetEdgar for my own use.

MeetEdgar allows you to have a library of content where you can decide when it goes out. You can easily see your schedule, what is in your library, and you can have the content go out again and again, which is great because you need to be telling people over and over again what you do! If you're using multiple platforms, that can get tiring.

Quick note – Twitter does not allow you to repost the same content more than once, so your Tweets need to be adapted slightly. I've found this can just be done with the addition of an emoji or hashtag!

Email marketing software

Mailchimp is my go-to here, as you know, but I've used others on behalf of clients. Choose the one that suits you best.

Having newsletters scheduled to go out automatically whenever someone joins my mailing list and while I am working away doing something else is a great feeling.

Mailchimp allows you to store all your email contacts, create newsletters, landing pages, integrate with various Plugins - including WooCommerce so you can see who's bought what. You can even see who's clicking links regularly, so that you can think about sending them an offer.

Don't forget; when you are in a position to invest in software, it can be offset as a business expense!

Emergency Planning

Sometimes, life gets in the way

~

As small business owners, we're in a very scary position if life decides to throw us an unexpected curve ball.

When I started my business, I'd already had two brain tumours removed, and just after I started out I was diagnosed with Addison's Disease, so I knew that life could throw things at you for no fair reason whatsoever.

I also know it's sometimes impossible to appreciate how life can take over if you've never been in that position, which is why I sometimes find it hard to help people realise that emergency planning is so very very important for a safe, sustainable and profitable business. It must be done before anything happens. It should not be something that falls down your to-do list to do 'tomorrow'.

What would you do if you suddenly had to close your laptop and disappear for a while (and I don't mean Robert Maxwell-style). Think more 'emergency' situations, like hospital stays, sick family members, a bereavement, a global pandemic!

I found myself in this position when I was told I needed imminent neurosurgery in late 2019.

I knew the tumour was back. The fatigue had got progressively worse and I'd lost the ability over time to run – which had been my escape for 10 years. My business was something I was so glad I didn't have to worry about.

Here are my top tried and tested tips to help you create a safe business and ensure you still have an income being generated, even if you can't work:

Have a team ready

You may not be able to afford to outsource at the moment, but there's nothing stopping you identifying a couple of people that you would trust to step in and take over your clients if you have to step out.

This could be a Virtual Business Manager, Virtual Assistant, or someone that runs the same business as you – someone you'd usually label as a 'competitor'. Ooooooh!

My team were my saviours when I had the news that my tumour was back for a third time and it was growing fast. I'd already built up relationships with them and we had a huge amount of respect for each other, so they were only too happy to help in any way they could. They were amazing.

Create a content log

Have all of your blogs listed in a spreadsheet, so you can share access to it with someone should you need to take time out. That someone can then keep your social media and newsletter presence up and running whilst you're, erm, neither up nor running! You know the importance of consistent marketing – we've been through that!

I use a content log for all of my blogs, testimonials, media and PR, so it's easy for me to schedule or hand over. It's so incredibly useful.

Head over to my YouTube channel for more content log tips.

Have an admin bible

This is somewhere where all your processes are typed up. Essentially, it's a plan of how to carry out every element of your day to day business.

I know that sounds like a right old pain, and possibly something that will stay on your to-do list for a long time without getting done, but imagine if you did have to take time out – now! You can easily email your admin bible to your Virtual Assistant, or someone else that you've identified to step in to cover your business during your emergency situation.

It's also a really good idea to have an admin bible for the work you may regularly do for any clients, so you can hand that over to someone else, too. Always have it checked and approved by the client, and store it safely at all times (good old GDPR).

The 20% Rule®

You know this off by heart now, right? No one client takes up more than 20% of your time – or your income.

When you have to take time out of your business, you'll be so surprised at how many people are happy to wait for you to return, or work with your substitute in the meantime. But, of course, not all of your clients will feel like that. If you're reliant on just a couple of people for your income, the odds might be against you, here.

Any clients who are happy to wait can do just that, and those who aren't could be outsourced to that team you've previously identified! Certainly don't give yourself more stress trying to appease those who take neither of those options.

Save like you're going to Vegas

Always have some money saved up, ideally to cover you for three months. Yes, this might mean no holidays one year, but how important is your business? Savings could mean you have so much less to worry about if you have to take emergency time out.

What I have also managed to do is save 15 months of money for anything really serious. Money I couldn't have saved on an employee's wage! That's not to brag – far from it. I say it as an incentive for you to consider putting money away every month. Even if it's just £25 at the beginning, that's all money aside for any emergencies. Or a massive holiday to Vegas if there are none!

Tell people

If something happens, don't be afraid to let your followers and audience know what's going on so that they can follow your journey. I found everyone to be incredibly supportive and it helped to get me back into it all when I was starting to feel a little more energetic and could come back to work.

Once you're a little better, tell your audience.

Take them on the journey with you so they don't forget about you.

Don't go underground and completely off radar, because you'll have to start all over again to build trust as well as presence on your return.

Create some passive income

Have a think about creating some form of passive income, so that you can earn even when you're not around. Here are some ideas.

- Write a book

- Write a course

- Write an eBook/resource

- Create a membership

- Sell pre-recorded webinars

- Join some affiliate schemes

- Create some merchandise

But remember, passive income isn't completely passive. You still need to tell people about it – all the time.

Don't forget; sometimes, life gets in the way.

Investing in You and Your Business

When someone wants what you offer,
I want people to think of you!

~

Should we invest in ourselves and our business? If you'd have asked me that question very early on in my business, I'd have said, *'Take the free stuff and learn from that.'*

What's the point in paying for anything when it's all out there for nothing on Google?

I was running my business, earning 'enough' to get by, and managing my life just fine, but I did have regular moments of stress and fear about 'what ifs'. I'd often wake at 4am and wonder if I was doing stuff right and if any of it was good enough for now or the future. I could see others going forward – not just VAs but other small business owners – and I wanted to move my business forward, too. The problem was, I didn't have a clue what to do or where to start. I was overwhelmed.

There was one thing all these other business owners had that I didn't, though – support from someone who had the experience. Someone who's already where they want to be. Someone they are accountable to!

Yeah, I'm accountable to Thames Water, British Gas and Swindon Borough Council, but funnily enough, they don't motivate me.

Like many self-employed people, I have no pension. I have health issues

– as I talked about at the start of this book – so life insurance is a no-no because it's so expensive. I have a daughter and I am her only biological provider. And, I have a goal to buy a holiday home in the next five years.

There's no way I could sustain a stress-free life and meet all my wants and needs just 'getting by'.

I knew where I wanted to be, but what was the most pain-free route? I didn't really want to go the scenic route, and that's not because I am impatient or don't want to put the time in. I'm a damn hard worker, but I don't want to make any costly mistakes or lose my business on the way, and that's what happens if you purely ingest all the free stuff. You can't possibly complete every five-day challenge, implement every bit of advice from a blog post, or watch others and believe you're doing everything right just from the perception they give.

Like you, I love what I do. I love my business and I wanted to make it work even better for me.

I know you know that free stuff is simply a lead magnet or part of someone's sales funnel. They don't create this free content because they're *simply passionate about helping other business owners succeed*. They – we – give the bare minimum to get the right audience interested, and then offer the full experience at a cost. After all, no one should give everything away for free – you, me and everyone else has to eat. We've got bills to pay and we deserve to enjoy life.

Around 2018, I invested in a membership just after publishing my first book, and it was quite an investment. I had been 'watching' the mentor for a while and could see how she was at business. I liked how she came across as a person, too. Her business was where I wanted to be, so it seemed like she was the perfect person to invest in. Still, I was scared. That's hard-earned money I was giving over to someone I hadn't actually met in real life.

It took a few weeks to get used to being 'around' other people and getting into a pattern of attending the membership's virtual events, but after a few months, the investment was recouped, simply by being around other business owners. They either worked with me themselves or would recommend me to others, because they'd got to know, like and trust me and I was becoming known for the services I provided.

Being with other business owners all wanting to succeed gives you an unimaginable amount of motivation. It makes you want to succeed, too.

I've learned not just to meet my goals but to smash them. I've learnt that I can shout about what I do and people will be pleased. The support from the community was unbelievable – because we were all on a similar journey.

And this is why, back in February 2019, I started my own membership programme, alongside running my own VA business, to support other virtual business owners to build and grow their business using the techniques I used in my own venture!

In 2020, I added an Expert Membership to my portfolio – for people already in business – where I share the techniques I use every day in my own business to help others reach their own specific goals to make their businesses safe, sustainable and profitable and become known as the expert so that when someone wants what you offer, people think of you. The programme is a way to work with me as your mentor in the most cost-effective way.

But is it just me who thinks investment pays off?

I asked some fellow business owners what they think about investing in their business versus binging on free resources, and have included a couple of replies here:

My business is now over six years old. When I started out, I gleaned information from free local workshops, YouTube videos, and trying and testing out various new methods. My business grew steadily but, if I am honest, maybe a little slowly. It was only when I started to invest in my business – both in terms of learning and buying software – that I really started to grow. I have bought online courses that cost nearly £1000, and I'm currently in about three different memberships – all for different reasons. I have invested in coaching, and earlier this year, invested in a mastermind. I have learned that when you put your money on the table, so to speak, that is when the gears start to shift. Not only are you invested financially, but I think it's a personal investment. As an entrepreneur, I see myself as worth investing in. I do think you should start off with baby steps, though. And when you do buy a course or a membership, make sure you use them!

– Louise Brogan

Without investment, I'd still be researching how to set up a business. When I find someone I resonate with, I love to soak up their content. What this does is confirm to me that they're an expert in their field. It gives me an indication of whether I'd like to invest in their paid services.

I know I need to invest. Being a business owner means that I feel I have to do everything within my business, and there are elements which naturally I'm not fully confident about. I need guidance, assistance, clarity, accountability – I need someone to help me get things done. You don't get this with free content. Investing in my business has enabled me to set up two businesses in the past three years. I have confidence in myself and know where I need to go for further development and help. I have a guide for my business. I've invested in excess of £5k in the last 3 years and an awful lot of time. I've spent the money so I want to see results. And I have. I can ask questions if need be. Memberships also give you a great business community to bounce ideas with and generally be around like-minded people who you can learn from.

– Fay Blakey

Between you and me, there did come a time just before renewal of my own subscription to the membership group where I thought, do you know what – I know how to set goals now. I've got consistent income, I sold copies of my first book beyond my wildest dreams, and I've pretty much nailed the marketing aspect of both businesses, so that's it for me, right?

Wrong!

What got me there wasn't just the advice from the mentor and peer support, it was knowing I was accountable because I'd said I'd do it and because I am my own biggest critic. Making sure my direction was focused and relevant to my business is so important.

I have new goals and I have places to go in business that I don't even know I want to visit yet, and the only way I'll know where I want to be is by watching other business owners, learning from them, watching their mistakes – so that I don't make them – and also utilising the experience and expertise of those around me.

I'm sure you sometimes struggle to find the time to go online – or wish you hadn't bothered when you find yourself in a three-hour scrolling cycle. That's why my own membership programme doesn't rely on you being on Facebook 24/7. Controversial, huh?

Here's some of what my members get for their monthly investment in my Expert Membership:

Accountability

To ensure you reach that expert level, you'll be encouraged to make weekly pledges on what you hope to achieve in the week ahead. Then, one of us will check-in midweek with you to see how you're getting on and support you where needed.

Expert's Hour

You, me and your fellow members will get together once every few weeks via Zoom to talk through everything and anything business related. From accountability and referrals, to growth planning and getting new clients, nothing is off the table and these sessions will inspire you to keep on track.

Power Hour

You'll receive one 60-minute 1:1 call with me (annual members) or one 20-minute 1:1 call with me (monthly members), so that I can see where you are and where you want to be, which will ensure that my advice and support is always relevant to you.

Expert Masterclasses

Regular sessions from myself and other industry experts will be held to teach you a range of skills that will help move your business forward. The best bit? You won't be sold to – you'll just be learning.

Access to Experts

Five days a week, myself and the team will be on hand in the private community (Facebook group and / or Slack – you choose which one you prefer to utilise) to help you keep focused and make progress. We're there to answer every question. Everything is relevant.

Expert Directory Listing

The biggest thing is to make you the expert; the person people go to when they need your specific service. So, you'll be added to an exclusive directory so that people can find you when they need what you sell.

Weekly Roundups

If you're busy being the expert and you're worried about missing any of the best bits, we've got that covered. At the end of every week, a roundup will be sent with a synopsis of what's happened and what's coming up for you – all to digest in your own time. It's your permission to pause.

Private Community Group

Facebook and Slack community groups for you to choose from – all content is replicated across both.

This is all focused purely on getting you where you want to be, whatever your individual goals are.

Together, you, me, the team and the other members will work together in regular calls. I'll send you tasks every week and you'll utilise the exclusive membership resources I've developed to help you complete them. These resources aren't lead magnets. They're focused on getting your service-based business to a safe, sustainable and profitable place – with no distractions.

But, programmes like this aren't just about the resources, they're about the community, too. Have a look online for my testimonials – and see for yourself the changes that are happening and the relationships that are forming.

I invite you to join my membership programme. You can find out more here: catherinegladwyn.co.uk/membership

Thank You

~

A massive thank you to the following people who pre-ordered a copy of this book before it was even finished. Thank you for believing in me. You're all flipping amazing.

To avoid squabbles my Mum gets first place:

Ann Gladwyn (My Mum!)

Carol Snelling

Jessica Jones

Natalie Smith

Jo Francis

Rachel Spencer

Susan Thomas

Gavin Reynoldson

Ilona Gierach

Karen Jansing

Sarah Clements

Gloria Holmes

Claire Atkinson

Christine Southam

Gemma Tanner

Naomi Spratt

Georgina Chapman

Lisa Porto

Amy Cook

Kelly Kemp

Yvonne Hemmings

Meg Small

Lyndsey Lee

Helen Porter

Iris Rusterholz

Yasmin Yarwood

Carole Searle

Kate Durrant

Catherine Cocklin

Lisa Heleniak

Dawn Roffe

Chrissy Silva

Mike Cottam

Olivia Vandyk

Rachael Curran

Katie Earl

Lorrayne Coombes

Sam Barratt

Gail Hawker

Nat Delfino

Diane Hudson

Louise Lewis

Tracey Robertson

Sam Chisman

Heidi Setchfield

Kelly McKenzie

Sarah Walton-Davey

Debbie Binnersley

Rachel Healy

Katherine Bryant

Wendy Griffith

Heather Cocks

Erica Agombar

Karen Gorham

Anh Ly

Karen Broughton

Catherine Berry

Samantha Bradbury

Alex Hughes

Pauleena Frederick

Louise Lloyd

Matthew Harris

Jo Cowlin

Rosemarie St Louis

Karen Tait

Catherine Pencavel

Sue Matthews

Louise Rigg

Fran Brinkworth

Amy Nolan

Marie Dunne

Kasia Kasperowicz

Marnie Wills

Tarsha Shaw

Marta Fernandez Cuendias

Amy Wells

Rhiannon Ford

Carey Vigor

Helen I'Anson

Jen Healy

Karima Akil

Natalie Trice

Laura Ball

Helen Lumber

Claudia Adams

Jack Harris

Kay Lundy

Kate Latham-Whitley

Lucy Griffin-Stiff

Nicolette Evans

Claire Reed

Hetty Verney

Michelle Counley

Rochelle Banton

Beverley Martin

Francisca Kozijn

Mahmood Reza

Dave down the chippy

PS: Stay up to date

You know full well that things can and do change so quickly, so make sure you don't have your head down too often, stuck in a cycle of one or a few elements of your business.

Look up every so often and keep learning.

That's it, I'm definitely going now...

References

forbes.com

jimsmarketingblog.com

gitomer.com

gov.uk

meetedgar.com

freeagent.com

zoom.us

Discounts

MeetEdgar: Get your first month free with my special link:
meetedgar.com/pricing/?via=z47wz

FreeAgent: Get 10% off and a 60 day free trial via this link:
freeagent.com/partners/delegateva/

PolicyBee for all your insurance needs.
Mention my name and get up to 10% off:
Catherine Gladwyn - Call: 0345 561 0320